intermediate

Reading/Writing

Module C

Based on materials taken from the following titles:

For Your Information 1: Basic Reading Skills, Karen Blanchard & Christine Root
For Your Information 2: Intermediate Reading Skills, Karen Blanchard & Christine Root
For Your Information 3: High-Intermediate Reading Skills, Karen Blanchard & Christine Root
Introduction to Academic Writing, Second Edition, Alice Oshima & Ann Hogue
More Reading Power: Reading for Pleasure, Comprehension Skills, Thinking Skills,
    Reading Faster, Beatrice S. Mikulecky & Linda Jeffries
Ready to Write More: From Paragraph to Essay, Karen Blanchard & Christine Root

PEARSON
Custom
Publishing

Excerpts taken from:

For Your Information 1: Basic Reading Skills,
by Karen Blanchard and Christine Root
Copyright © 1996 by Addison Wesley Longman, Inc.
A Pearson Education Company
White Plains, NY 10606
ISBN: 0-201-83409-X

For Your Information 2: Intermediate Reading Skills,
by Karen Blanchard and Christine Root
Copyright © 1996 by Addison Wesley Longman, Inc.
ISBN: 0-201-82538-4

For Your Information 3: High-Intermediate Reading Skills,
by Karen Blanchard and Christine Root
Copyright © 1997 by Addison Wesley Longman, Inc.
ISBN: 0-201-87798-8

Introduction to Academic Writing, Second Edition,
by Alice Oshima and Ann Hogue
Copyright © 1997 by Addison Wesley Longman, Inc.
ISBN: 0-201-69509-X

Ready to Write More: From Paragraph to Essay,
by Karen Blanchard and Christine Root
Copyright © 1997 by Addison Wesley Longman, Inc.
ISBN: 0-201-87807-0

More Reading Power: Reading for Pleasure, Comprehension Skills, Thinking Skills, Reading Faster,
by Beatrice S. Mikulecky and Linda Jeffries
Copyright © 1996 by Addison Wesley Longman, Inc.
ISBN: 0-201-60970-3

This special edition published in cooperation with Pearson Custom Publishing.

Printed in the United States of America

10 9 8 7 6 5 4 3 2 1

ISBN 0-536-74479-3

BA 997989

DG

Please visit our web site at *www.pearsoncustom.com*

PEARSON CUSTOM PUBLISHING
75 Arlington Street, Suite 300, Boston, MA 02116
A Pearson Education Company

TABLE OF CONTENTS

Thematic Reading Section: The World of Business

Writing Section

Thematic Reading: Human Behavior

Writing Section

ACKNOWLEDGMENTS

On behalf of ELS Education Services, Inc., I would like to express our thanks to the 2001 Curriculum Project Team, Margene Petersen, Ward Morrow, Donn Callaway, Ellen Clegg, Mary Hernandez, and Dan Manolescu, for their contributions of time, knowledge, experience, and practical perspective.

Thanks to Susan Matson, Marjorie Friedman, and Terri Rapoport for their insightful comments in the initial curriculum design and textbook selection process.

Thanks to Sheryl Olinsky Borg for encouragement and focus on the process.

Thanks to Judy Judd-Price for relentless enforced compliance with deadlines and for taking this project from concept to reality.

And, special thanks to all of the Academic Directors, faculty, and students of ELS Language Centers who piloted the earlier texts and gave us invaluable feedback . . . the voice of our customers.

A job well done by all.

Mark W. Harris
President and CEO
ELS Language Centers

INTRODUCTION

We at ELS Language Centers are proud to present our new Intermediate Reading and Writing textbooks. These books are used for a portion of the day in our Intensive English programs and are complemented by texts and materials in Structure and Speaking Practice, Conversation, Multi-Media Lab and Elective classes. There are three stages in the ELS Language Centers Reading and Writing curricullum—Beginning, Intermediate and Advanced—and each stage consists of three levels of achievement, low to high.

In developing this series, the focus has been on promoting active rather than passive readers and writers through the practice of reading, summarizing, sharing, and reflecting through responding both orally and in written form.

In designing these texts, we used a vareity of resources to provide learners with authentic readings of high interest and appeal, with various tasks to improve reading comprehension and speed, and through topics that stimulate discussion and thought. These texts also include various resources to provide learners models of writing, clear explanations and practice of grammatical structures and mechanics, as well as a variety of rhetorical styles to develop written communication.

Each text consists of two themes that provide the learner with numerous activities.

- To promote active reading
- To enhance critical thinking
- To increase reading comprehension, including understanding vocabulary in context
- To stimulate discussion and reflection
- To develop summary/response skills, orally and written
- To develop more effective written communication, including learning rhetorical styles and editing for incorrect use of grammar structures and mechanics
- To grow organizational thought

These activities are tasks that the students complete in pairs, groups, and individually. Some activities require that after summarizing an article, students share the information with others who have not read the same material. As a result, students have a purpose for reading and can actively share what they know and have learned. The role of the instructor is to create a positive environment in which students are encouraged to understand unfamiliar vocabulary, are stimulated to discuss a variety of topics and ideas and empowered to share what they have learned. The instructor also has the role of monitoring students' progress and giving corrective feedback throughout each session.

THEMATIC READING SECTION

The World of Business

UNIT 1

Companies with a Conscience

SELECTION 1

An <u>entrepreneur</u> is a person who owns and runs a business. Entrepreneurs develop creative new ideas and bring them to the marketplace. Anita Roddick is a <u>successful</u> entrepreneur who owns and runs The Body Shop, a company that sells naturally based products for skin and hair. This unusual company is the subject of the following article: **Profits with Principles**.

Profits with Principles

1   Anita Roddick, founder of The Body Shop, was trained as a school teacher. She didn't know anything about the cosmetics industry when she opened her first small shop in Brighton, England, in 1976. But she had good ideas, and people liked her products. Her business grew quickly. Because of her energy, determination, and vision, Anita Roddick has become an international success story. She is one of the five richest women in England. Today, there are over 1,300 <u>branches</u> of The Body Shop in forty-five countries around the world.

2   The Body Shop manufactures and sells over 400 different naturally based products. Anita learns how people from traditional cultures use plants and herbs from their <u>environment</u> to take care of their bodies. In Sri Lanka, for example, she learned that women <u>rub</u> fresh pineapple on their skin to make it softer and smoother. With that <u>knowledge</u>, she created a face product using pineapple. In Polynesia, she learned about many of the uses of cocoa

Profits with Principles. SOURCES: "Anita Roddick" by Pope Brock, *People Magazine*, May 10, 1993, pages 101–106; "The Body Shop International" Harvard Business School Case # 9-392-032. Harvard Business School, Boston, MA, 02163, pages 1–9.

butter. It makes the skin softer and the hair shinier. Cocoa Butter Hand and Body Lotion is one of The Body Shop's best-selling products.

3   The philosophy of The Body Shop is different from the philosophy of most cosmetics companies. It does not promise miracles or everlasting youth. The Body Shop develops its line of high-quality, sensible products by using traditional wisdom, herbal knowledge, and modern technology. *seduction*

4   The Body Shop does not believe in profits without principles. A respect for the environment is one of The Body Shop's most basic principles. The company uses as little packaging as possible to conserve natural resources and reduce waste. Customers are encouraged to bring their old containers to the shop to refill them. If they do this, they get a discount on their next purchase. The Body Shop is also strongly opposed to animal testing in the cosmetics industry. It never tests its products or ingredients on animals.

5   Helping communities in need is another principle. All employees are encouraged to do volunteer work with local groups. The Body Shop gives employees four hours off each month to do their community work. Some projects include working with homeless people and AIDS victims. The Body Shop also provides educational programs for its staff and customers.

6   The Body Shop has set up trade partnerships with communities in need around the world. "Trade Not Aid" is a cornerstone[1] of the company. For example, The Body Shop has made an agreement with the Kayapo Indians, who harvest Brazil nuts in the Amazon rain forest. The Body Shop uses these nuts in one of its products, Brazil Nut Oil Conditioner for hair. The agreement has several goals. One is to protect the plants the Kayapo Indians harvest from the rain forest. Another goal is to make sure that the Kayapo get the economic benefits from any commercial development in their area. There are similar agreements with communities in India, Mexico, Nepal, Tanzania, and

7   Zambia.

Although some of Anita Roddick's ideas for The Body Shop seem unusual for the business world, she must be doing something right. In 1994/5, The Body Shop's international profits were over $34 million.

How Well Did You Read?

Read the following statements. If a statement is true, write T *on the line. If it is false, write* F.

___F___   **1.** Anita Roddick studied business in school.

___T___   **2.** The Body Shop is a very successful business.

___T___   **3.** Many of the ideas for The Body Shop's products come from traditional cultures around the world.

___F___   **4.** The philosophy of The Body Shop is similar to the philosophies of most other cosmetics companies.

___T___   **5.** One of The Body Shop's most important principles is respecting the environment.

[1]**cornerstone** Something of great importance.

Building Reading Skills

Scanning for Details

Read the following questions about The Body Shop. Then scan the article to find the answers. Work as quickly as possible. Do not read every word in the article. As soon as you find the answer to a question, move on to the next one.

1. When did the first Body Shop open? _She opened her First small shop in 1976._

2. How many branches of The Body Shop are there in the world today? _There are over 1300 Branches of the body shop._

3. How many countries have branches of The Body Shop? _FORTY-FIve countries around the world._

4. Approximately how many kinds of products does The Body Shop make and sell? _Approximately 400 Kinds of Products_

5. Where did Anita learn about the uses of cocoa butter? _She learn about the uses of cocoa Butter in Polinesia_

6. Where do the Kayapo Indians live? _Kayapo indians live in Brazil_

7. What were The Body Shop's recent international profits in 1994/5? _The body shop's Recent international ProFits were over 34$ million_

Talk it Over

Discussion

1. Why do you think The Body Shop has become so successful?

2. How does Anita Roddick get ideas for The Body Shop's products? Do you think this is a good way? Why or why not?

3. How is the philosophy of The Body Shop different from that of most other cosmetics companies? Do you agree with The Body Shop's philosophy? Why or why not?

4. In what ways does The Body Shop show its respect and concern for the environment?

5. What types of things does The Body Shop do to help communities in need?

6. What do you think "Trade Not Aid" means?

Expanding Vocabulary

Circle the letter of the word that best completes each sentence.

1. The Body Shop is part of the _____ industry.
   a. traditional
   b. cosmetics
   c. environment

2. The company tries to _____ natural resources by using as little packaging as possible.
   a. conserve
   b. spend
   c. oppose

3. Many of the _____ for The Body Shop's products come from different countries around the world.
   a. goals
   b. cultures
   c. ingredients

4. The Body Shop _____ over 400 kinds of skin and hair products.
   a. manufactures
   b. buys
   c. protects

5. The Body Shop _____ the use of animals for testing in the cosmetics industry.
   a. trains
   b. opposes
   c. believes in

6. Customers who use The Body Shop's products do not expect _____ .
   a. miracles
   b. wisdom
   c. profits

7. Many of The Body Shop's employees do _____ work in their communities.
   a. commercial
   b. traditional
   c. volunteer

8. When customers bring in their old _____ to the shop for refills, they get a discount.
   a. products
   b. containers
   c. cosmetics

9. One goal of The Body Shop's trade partnerships is to _____ the Amazon rain forest.
   a. oppose
   b. manufacture
   c. protect

SELECTION 2

Mitch Curren is the Coordinator of Public Relations for Ben & Jerry's, a successful ice cream company in Burlington, Vermont. In the following interview, **The Scoop on Ben & Jerry's,** Ms. Curren talks about some of the ways that Ben & Jerry's is unique.

Before You Read

Prereading Activity

Look at this excerpt from the cover of Ben & Jerry's: The Inside Scoop, *by Fred Lager. Then answer the questions that follow with your classmates.*

In 1978, with a total investment of $12,000, Ben Cohen and Jerry Greenfield opened a homemade ice cream parlor in an abandoned gas station in Burlington, Vermont, and set out to serve the best ice cream they could make. Less than 15 years later, Ben & Jerry's has grown into a national phenomenon, with annual sales of over $100 million.

But Ben & Jerry's wasn't just another success story, it was a whole new kind of company. First, the founders believed that work should be rewarding in itself. Their unofficial motto was, "If it's not fun, why do it?" Second, they believed that business should give something back to the community that supports it. They started by giving away free ice cream and sponsoring local festivals, but as the company grew, their efforts became more ambitious, and Ben & Jerry's was soon recognized as one of the most progressive, socially active companies in America.

1. What do you think Ben and Jerry meant by their motto, "If it's not fun, why do it?" Do you think this was a good motto for a new business? Why or why not?

2. Do you agree with the idea that business should give something back to the community that supports it?

The Scoop on Ben & Jerry's

How did Ben & Jerry's get started?

1   Ben Cohen and Jerry Greenfield have been friends since they were in seventh grade. That was in 1963. In 1977, they decided to start an ice cream business together. They took a $5 course to learn how to make ice cream. Then, they opened their first ice cream parlor in Burlington, Vermont, in 1978. Jerry's job was to make the ice cream and to make sure it tasted better than anybody else's ice cream. Ben's job was to sell the ice cream and make sure that everyone knew that Ben & Jerry's ice cream was the best ice cream in the world.

2   They both ate a lot of their ice cream because that was the best way to figure out how good it was. They tried different things and experimented with unusual flavors and recipes for their ice cream. They decided to make ice cream flavors with lots of big chunks of cookies, candies, fruits, and nuts. Ben and Jerry's ideas, and their rich, creamy, chunky ice cream made their business very popular, very fast.

What made Ben & Jerry's such a big success?

3   Ben and Jerry figured out the secret to making great ice cream. They started with fresh milk and cream and added lots of natural flavorings, lots of big chunks, and lots of imagination. To get people to try their product, Ben and Jerry gave out free samples of ice cream everywhere they went. Their plan worked. The more ice cream they gave away, the more new customers they got.

5   Ben and Jerry wanted to run their business with goals that were different from the goals of traditional businesses. Traditional businesses usually have one main goal—to make a lot of money. Ben & Jerry's has three main goals: to make great products, to make money, and to share that money with the community. Ben and Jerry believe that as business prospers, the community prospers too. They call this idea "linked prosperity."

The average North American eats about 32 quarts (35.2 liters) of ice cream per year.

What makes Ben & Jerry's such an unusual business?

5   Our belief that all businesses have a responsibility to give something back to their communities was a very unusual idea several years ago when we first started talking about it. Some people thought we were crazy. They told us that no business could ever succeed and make big profits if it kept giving away the profits to the community. We decided to try it and soon we were able to prove that we weren't as crazy as people thought.

6   Here are some examples of things we've done and are still doing. First of all, every year we give away 7.5 percent of our pretax profits to groups working for the needs of their community. So far, we've given away more than $3 million. But we feel like we've just begun! We also give away lots of ice cream every year. We donate it to charitable groups, food shelves,[1] and community events. In addition, we buy our ingredients from suppliers whose business goals are a lot like ours. For example, we get our brownies from a bakery that employs formerly homeless men and

The Scoop on Ben & Jerry's. Interview printed with the permission of Mitch Curren, Coordinator of Public Relations for Ben & Jerry's.

[1]**food shelves** Places where food is free for people who need it.

people recovering from drug and alcohol addiction. We get our coffee flavorings from a special cooperative[2] run by Mexican farmers. We buy our cookie dough chunks from another socially responsible company in Vermont.

What else do you do that makes Ben & Jerry's a special kind of company?

7 Well, Ben & Jerry's employees love a good party. So, every year we have huge parties called "One World, One Heart Festivals." This is our way of thanking all our customers while celebrating with them. Tens of thousands of people come to our free festivals to listen to famous musical groups, to eat our ice cream, and to join us in "Social Action Campaigns." These Social Action Campaigns encourage the U.S. government to spend more money on programs that help people who are in need.

Building Reading Skills

Identifying Main Ideas

Which of the following topics are discussed in the interview? Put a check mark next to those topics.

_____ **1.** how Ben and Jerry got people to try their product

_____ **2.** the company's main goals

_____ **3.** Ben & Jerry's competition

_____ **4.** examples of the company's social action

_____ **5.** the company's history

_____ **6.** the nutritional value of Ben & Jerry's ice cream

How Well Did You Read?

Match each topic with its explanation. Write the correct letter on the line.

TOPIC	EXPLANATION
_____ **1.** Ben's job	**a.** start with fresh milk and cream, lots of natural flavorings, lots of big chunks, lots of imagination
_____ **2.** Ben & Jerry's main goals	**b.** to make ice cream and make sure it tasted great
_____ **3.** Ben & Jerry's secret	**c.** sharing money with the community so as the business prospers, the community prospers too
_____ **4.** Jerry's job	**d.** to make great products, to make money, and to find ways to share that money with the community
_____ **5.** linked prosperity	**e.** Ben and Jerry's great ideas and rich, creamy, chunky ice cream
_____ **6.** what made Ben & Jerry's very popular, very fast	**f.** to sell the ice cream and make sure everyone knew it was great

[2]**cooperative** An organization owned by the people who use it and work in it

Building Vocabulary Skills

Vocabulary in Context

With a partner, try to guess the meaning of the underlined words. Use the information in the sentences to figure out the meaning. Do not use your dictionary. Circle the letter of the word or phrase that is closest in meaning to the underlined word in each sentence.

1. They tried different things and <u>experimented with</u> unusual flavors and recipes for their ice cream.
   a. bought
   b. tried
   c. threw away

2. They decided to make ice cream flavors with lots of big <u>chunks</u> of cookies, candies, fruits, and nuts.
   a. pieces
   b. copies
   c. bowls

3. To get people to try their product, Ben and Jerry gave out free <u>samples</u> of ice cream everywhere they went. . . . The more ice cream they gave away, the more new customers they got.
   a. small amounts to taste
   b. something to buy
   c. an unusual idea

4. Ben & Jerry's has three main goals: to make great products, to make money, and to share that money with the community. Ben and Jerry believe that as business <u>prospers</u>, the community <u>prospers</u> too.
   a. responds
   b. grows weak
   c. becomes successful

5. We also give away lots of ice cream every year. We <u>donate</u> it to charitable groups, food shelves, and community events.
   a. buy
   b. give
   c. sell

 The best-selling flavor of Ben & Jerry's ice cream is chocolate chip cookie dough, with approximately 9.6 million pints (5,285,760 liters) sold annually.

SELECTION 3

Patagonia is an outdoor clothing company that was started in the 1960s by Yvon Chouinard, an entrepreneur with a vision. In **Warm and Fuzzy Soda Bottles**, you will read about how Patagonia is committed to helping the environment.

Before You Read

Prereading Questions

1. Do you enjoy outdoor activities such as rock climbing, running, sailing, hiking, or biking? If so, which ones?

2. Based on the title, "Warm and Fuzzy Soda Bottles," what do you think the article might be about? Take a guess. You may be surprised.

Warm and Fuzzy Soda Bottles

1   Yvon Chouinard loves the outdoors. He surfs, climbs rocks, skis, hikes, kayaks, and runs Patagonia, a multimillion dollar company. Although Mr. Chouinard does all of these things very well, his real passion is saving the earth. In fact, Mr. Chouinard says he had two reasons for starting his company. First, he wanted to earn enough money so he could become an active environmental philanthropist.[1] And second, he wanted the freedom to spend as much time as possible enjoying nature.

2   Patagonia designs and distributes clothing for use in extreme outdoor weather conditions. It originally started in the 1960s as a climbing and mountaineering equipment company. Yvon Chouinard used to manufacture climbing hardware and sell it out of the back of his car up in the mountains. He then moved on to selling clothing for use in the mountains. All of his products continue to be designed for comfort, simplicity, and versatility.

3   Mr. Chouinard's business grew rapidly, and in 1994, its sales reached $125 million. Patagonia's clothing is popular because it is versatile, comfortable, dries quickly, and remains warm even when it is wet. It works well in hot, cold, wet, dry, humid, arid, windy, and calm weather. Patagonia products are sold around the world through its mail-order catalog.

4   In addition to its commitment to providing high-quality products to its customers, Patagonia is also committed to the environment. It pledges one percent of its sales each year to the preservation and restoration of the natural environment. With recent annual sales of $125 million, the company gave $1.2 million to environmental groups around the world.

5   In the early 1990s, Patagonia acknowledged in its catalog that every product Patagonia designed and distributed polluted the earth in some way. The company decided to decrease the impact of its products on the environment and to help people learn more about environmental problems. As a result, in the fall of 1993, Patagonia introduced a new product, a sweater made of recycled soda bottles! The warm, soft, fuzzy fabric was called PCR (Post-Consumer Recycled) Synchilla™. (*Post-consumer recycled* refers to products that have been used by people before.) Because soda bottles are made from very high-quality plastic, it is possible to melt the bottles and make them into yarn for clothes.

6   It takes twenty-five two-liter bottles to make each sweater. The result is that for each sweater made, twenty-five fewer soda bottles go into a landfill[2] somewhere. In addition, it takes less energy and fewer natural resources to make PCR Synchilla™ than it does to make virgin (new) polyester. The first sweaters were made of 80 percent PCR-Synchilla™ and 20 percent virgin polyester. Within a year, the technology had improved and the ratio became 90 percent PCR-Synchilla™ and 10 percent virgin polyester in some products. This meant that more soda bottles were needed to produce an item, so fewer bottles went into landfills. Patagonia's PCR-Synchilla™ products

Warm and Fuzzy Soda Bottles. From a letter written by Lu Setnika, Public Affairs Director for Patagonia. Reprinted with the permission of Lu Setnika.
[1]**philanthropist** Someone who gives a lot of money to charity.
[2]**landfill** A place where trash is buried.

help people see and understand the positive results of recycling. In fact, Patagonia was so determined to share this new technology that it did not patent[3] the process. It hopes that other companies will also use it.

7   In addition to innovations in the technology of making fabrics, Patagonia has also been urging people to simplify their lives and recycle clothes they don't need. The company tries to make its products as multifunctional as possible. For example, rather than having one pair of shorts to play volleyball in and four other pairs for basketball, kayaking, hiking, and running, Patagonia offers one pair which can be used in a variety of sports under a variety of conditions. This means more space in your closet and less trash in landfills.

8   Patagonia is committed to sharing the issue of environmental responsibility with other businesses. Mr. Chouinard, the board of directors, and the employees think of the company as a tool for social change. It is their hope that more companies will recognize the environmental "costs" of doing business and try to be more planet-friendly.

Building Skills

Identifying Main Ideas

In small groups, make a list of the main ideas of the article. Then write your lists on the chalkboard and compare them.

_____

_____

_____

Building Reading Skills

Scanning for Details

Read the following questions about Patagonia. Then scan the article to find the answers. Try to work quickly. Do not reread every word in the article. As soon as you find the answer to a question, move on to the next one.

1. Who owns Patagonia? ___IVON Chouinard is Patagonia's OWNER___

2. What did the company sell in the 1960s? ___The company sell climbing and MOUNTAINEERING equipment in the 1960.___

3. When did Patagonia's sales reach $125 million? ___Patagonia's sales $125 million in 1994. Reach.___

4. Why is Patagonia's clothing popular? ___because the clothing it is versatile, comfortable, dries quickly, and remains warm.___

5. What percent of its sales does Patagonia give to environmental causes? ___Patagonia give to environmental causes one percent of its sales each year.___

[3]**patent** To protect from being copied or sold by those who do not have a right to do so

6. How many two-liter bottles does it take to make one PCR-Synchilla™ sweater? _____To make one_
PCR synchilla ᵗⁿ sweater You need 2 Twenty Five, two liter Bottles

7. What percent of virgin polyester was used in the first PCRSynchilla™ sweaters? _____The First PCR_
Sinchilla ᵗⁿ sweater was used 20 Percent of virgin Polyester.

How Well Did You Read?

Patagonia is committed to designing practical clothing that does not have a negative impact on the environment. The following statements describe the reasons behind and the results of some of Patagonia's work.

1. Read this list of reasons:

- Patagonia wanted to decrease the impact of its products on the environment.
- Patagonia wants people to simplify their lives.
- It takes twenty-five two-liter bottles to make each PCR-Synchilla™ sweater.
- Patagonia's clothes are versatile and comfortable.
- Patagonia does not intend to patent the process for making fabric from soda bottles.
- Patagonia improved the technology for making PCR-Synchilla™.
- Patagonia is committed to the environment.

2. Read the list of results that have been written in the result spaces below.

3. Decide which reason from above led to each result below. Write the correct reason in the appropriate reason arrow.

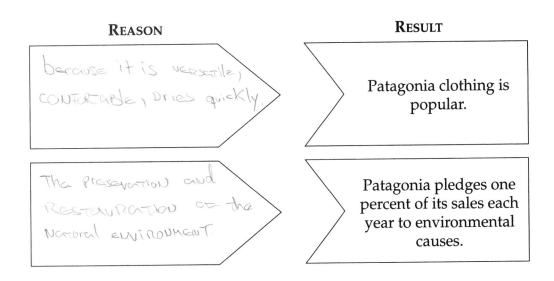

REASON	RESULT
because it is versatile, comfortable, Dries quickly.	Patagonia clothing is popular.
The Preservation and Restauration of the Natural Environment.	Patagonia pledges one percent of its sales each year to environmental causes.

REASON	RESULT
	Patagonia developed PCR-Synchilla™ to use in making sweaters.
	Fewer bottles go into landfills.
	Other companies will be able to use it.
	Patagonia products are as multifunctional as possible.
	The new ratio for PCR-Synchilla™ is 9 to 1.

FYI It is estimated that **45** percent of **North Americans** recycle bottles and cans, but they consume the equivalent of five times their own weight in paper annually.

Read and React

Read the following statements made by Yvon Chouinard. Then in small groups, discuss your reactions to them.

1. "The measly million or so that we're giving away each year isn't very much money. But I think we're having a tremendous influence on other corporations."[1]

2. "I don't think corporate America realizes how serious people are about the environment. They're scared to death."[2]

3. "Civilization is out of control, growing way beyond its resources, and it will destroy itself."[3]

Building Vocabulary Skills

Synonyms or Antonyms

Decide if the following pairs of words are synonyms or antonyms. If they are synonyms, circle S. If they are antonyms, circle A.

1. versatile	multifunctional	(S)	A
2. humid	arid	S	(A)
3. pledge *Prometer*	promise	(S)	A
4. impact	effect	(S)	A
5. extensive	limited	S	(A)
6. recognize → *Reconocer*	realize → *Realizar - Darse cuenta*	(S)	A
7. ratio → *Proporción*	proportion	(S)	A
8. committed - *Cometer - Comprometerse* dedicated		(S)	A

Building Vocabulary Skills

Prefixes

Another prefix that is commonly used in English is *re-*. When *re-* is put in front of a verb, it usually means *to do something again*. For example, the word *rebuild* means to build again:

> We had to <u>rebuild</u> our house after the earthquake.

---

[1] *The Chronicle of Philanthropy,* June 1, 1993, p. 10.
[2] *The Chronicle of Philanthropy,* June 1, 1993, p. 12.
[3] *Los Angeles Times,* Jan. 28, 1994.

In this unit, you have seen the prefix *re-* several times:

1. Customers are encouraged to bring their old containers to the shop to <u>refill</u> them.

2. Patagonia has also been urging people to simplify their lives and <u>recycle</u> clothes they don't need.

You have done many vocabulary exercises in this book. Now it is your turn to create some. In small groups, talk about the definition of each of the following words. Then write a vocabulary exercise using the words in the list. When you have finished, give your exercise to another group to complete.

reprint   redecorate   rearrange   refuel   reread

Building Vocabulary Skills

Word Forms

Complete each sentence with the correct word.

1. ambitious   ambition

    a. You need a lot of _____ to start your own business.

    b. Anita Roddick is a very _____ person.

2. imagine   imagination

    a. It took a lot of hard work and _____ to complete this project.

    b. Can you _____ a world without poverty and war?

3. progress   progressive

    a. He is working hard and making a lot of _____ on his research.

    b. This is a very _____ school. It uses the most modern teaching methods.

4. responsible   responsibility

    a. It is your _____ to remember to do all your assignments on time.

    b. I really trust my babysitter; she is very _____ .

5. celebration   celebrate

    a. We had a big _____ when our son graduated from high school.

    b. I won the lottery. Let's _____ !

6. encourage   encouragement

    a. Children need a lot of _____ , especially when they are trying something new.

    b. Teachers should _____ their students to be creative thinkers.

7. conserve   conservation

    a. It is important to _____ resources like water and electricity.

    b. Many governments believe in the _____ of their country's wildlife.

8. oppose   opposition

    a. We _____ the city's plan to cut down so many trees.

    b. There is a lot of _____ to the university's plan to raise tuition.

9. protect   protection

    a. These boots are good _____ against rain and snow.

    b. Mothers and fathers try to _____ their young children.

10. preserve   preservation

    a. We are committed to the _____ of our environment.

    b. It is important to _____ our valuable natural resources.

11. distributes   distribution

    a. The company _____ its products in many countries.

    b. Who is responsible for the _____ of the prizes?

12. versatile   versatility

    a. Plastic is a _____ material.

    b. She is known for her _____ as a performer.

13. comfort   comfortable

    a. My shoes are very _____ .

    b. I buy my shoes for _____ rather than style.

14. environment   environmental

    a. We need to learn more about _____ problems.

    b. Everyone should be concerned about the _____ .

How Well Did You Read?

The three companies you read about sell different products, but they share some of the same goals. Read the following list and write the name of the company that each item applies to. Some statements may be true for more than one company, and others may not be true for any of them. If the statement does not apply to any of the three companies, leave it blank.

The Body Shop • Ben & Jerry's • Patagonia

_____   **1.** makes and sells ice cream

_____   **2.** opened its first shop in England

_____   **3.** sells its products in many countries

_____   **4.** manufactures and sells cosmetics

_____   **5.** gives away lots of free samples

_____   **6.** uses soda bottles to make sweaters

_____   **7.** uses natural ingredients

_____   **8.** operates like a traditional business

_____   **9.** is committed to helping the environment

_____   **10.** designs and distributes clothing

_____   **11.** opened its first shop in Vermont

_____   **12.** sponsors festivals to thank customers

_____   **13.** believes that business should give something back to the community that supports it

_____   **14.** promises miracles for those who use its products

ABOVE MATERIAL FROM: FOR YOUR INFORMATION 1

UNIT 2

Getting Down to Business

SELECTION 1

Blue jeans are very popular with people of all ages and nationalities. Look around your classroom. How many people are wearing jeans? In **Levi's Gold** you will read about Levi Strauss, the man who first introduced jeans.

Before You Read

Prereading Activity

1. What are some of the most popular brands of blue jeans in your country? Is Levi's a popular brand in your country?
2. What are some places where it is appropriate to wear jeans in your country? Are there some places where you wouldn't wear jeans? For example, would you wear jeans to work, school, a nice restaurant, church?
3. Before you read the article, discuss the meaning of the following words and phrases with your classmates:

| gold rush | patent | canvas |
| prospector | peddle | entrepreneur |

First Reading

Skimming

Read the article one time quickly, and look for the main idea. That is, skim the article.

Levi's Gold

DOROTHY SLATE

1   When the clipper ship sailed through California's Golden Gate[1] that March day in 1853, twenty-four-year-old Levi Strauss rushed to the deck, eager to see San Francisco. The Gold Rush[2], started in 1848, still drew men by the thousands to seek their fortunes. Strauss was one of them.

2   Six years earlier, he had left Bavaria in Germany to escape unfair laws against Jews and to join his older brothers Jonas and Louis in New York. They taught him English and told him peddling was an honorable occupation in the United States. Now he faced a new challenge. In his baggage were goods to sell. His brothers had helped select them in New York before he left on his long voyage around Cape Horn to California. Gold miners were sure to need thread, needles, scissors, thimbles, and rolls of canvas cloth for tents and wagon covers.

3   As Strauss looked toward the city, he saw several small boats approaching the ship. When they came close, some of their passengers clamored for news from the East. Others climbed aboard to see what merchandise the ship had brought. In a short while, Strauss had sold almost everything he had brought with him. Only the rolls of canvas remained.

4   Stepping ashore, he saw a bustling city with many "stores" that were merely tents or shanties. Among the ironworks, billiard-table manufacturers, dry-goods stores, breweries, and hundreds of saloons stood some stranded ships serving as hotels.

5   With gold dust from his sales aboard ship, Strauss bought a cart. He loaded his rolls of canvas and pushed the cart along wood-planked sidewalks. He parked on Montgomery Street, waiting for miners to pass by.

6   A prospector stopped to look at his canvas.

7   "It's for tenting," Strauss explained.

8   "Shoulda brought pants," the prospector told him. "Pants don't wear worth a hoot in the diggin's. Can't get a pair strong enough to last."

9   Instantly, the young entrepreneur sought out a tailor and created the first pair of jeans. Pleased with them, his customer later strutted around San Francisco. "Doggone, if a man ever had a pair of pants strong as Levi's before," he said.

10 The demand for "Levi's" grew so fast that Strauss could hardly keep up with it. When the brown canvas was gone, he switched to a sturdy fabric, *serge de Nîmes,* from Nîmes, France. The name was quickly shortened to "denim," and Strauss adopted the indigo blue familiar today.

[1]**Golden Gate**   The entrance to San Francisco Bay in northern California from the Pacific Ocean.
[2]**Gold Rush**   Gold was discovered in California in the late 1840s. As a result, many people rushed to California, hoping to find gold and become rich.

11   Levi's brothers Jonas and Louis were his partners, as was David Stern, who had married Levi's sister Fanny. They decided to call their firm Levi Strauss & Company, agreeing that Levi was the "business head" in the family. Years went by, and the business grew.

12   Then, in July 1872, a letter arrived from Jacob W. Davis, a tailor in Reno. The letter explained that he was now reinforcing pants pocket corners with copper rivets. Rivets strengthened the seams, which tore out when miners and other workers stuffed their pockets with gold nuggets and tools.

13   Davis was flooded with orders but worried that someone would steal his idea. If Levi Strauss & Company would take out a patent in his name, Davis would give them half the right to sell the riveted clothing.

14   Strauss immediately saw the profit potential. Instead of nine or ten dollars a dozen, the riveted pants could bring thirty-six dollars just for adding a penny's worth of metal. It was a good risk.

15   The U.S. Patent Office took its time in granting Strauss a patent. It took ten months and many revisions and amendments before the Patent Office agreed that the idea of riveted pockets was unusual enough to be patented.

16   When Davis moved his family to San Francisco, Strauss put him in charge of production. Soon a force of sixty women stitched Levi's on a piecework basis. The orange thread still used today was an attempt to match the copper rivets. Another still-used trademark is the leather label featuring two teamsters whipping a pair of horses trying to tear apart the riveted pants.

17   Successful in business, Levi Strauss still found time to participate in many civic organizations and was well liked in San Francisco's business community. He never married, saying, "I am a bachelor, and I fancy on that account I need to work more, for my entire life is my business."

18   Although he had no children of his own, Strauss established many scholarships at the University of California, and when he died in 1902, he left money to Protestant, Catholic, and Jewish orphanages. He left the business to his sister Fanny's children.

19   Levi Strauss found gold not in streams or mines, but in fulfilling an everyday need. Today presidents, movie stars, and millions of other people wear Levi's and other brands of jeans, clothing created by an entrepreneur who responded to the needs of the market.

Identifying the Main Idea

Circle the letter of the statement that best expresses the main idea of the passage.

a.   Gold miners bought Levi's pants because they were strong and durable.

b.   Levi Strauss was able to make his fortune in jeans by responding to the needs of the market.

c.   Levi was the "business head" of the Strauss family.

d.   Levi Strauss was successful in business, but he still found time to participate in civic organizations.

Second Reading

Now reread "Levi's Gold" and do the exercises that follow.

How Well Did You Read?

Read the following statements. If a statement is true, write T *on the line. If it is false, write* F.

_____ **1.** Levi's pants became popular very quickly.

_____ **2.** Levi brought canvas cloth to San Francisco to sell pants to the gold miners.

_____ **3.** Levi Strauss & Co. was a family business.

_____ **4.** The U.S. Patent Office quickly granted the patent for riveted pockets.

_____ **5.** Levi thought of using copper rivets to reinforce pocket corners.

Recalling Information

How Much Can You Remember?

Complete the paragraph with information from the article. See how much you can do without referring to the article. You do not have to use the exact words from the article as long as the idea is correct.

Levi Strauss went to _____ in 1853 in search of _____ , but ended up making his fortune in _____ . He realized that a good way to make money was to make and sell _____ _____ that were suited for a _____ lifestyle. His new business was very _____ , and soon many people were buying his _____ . In 1872, he made another good business decision; he added _____ to his pant's pocket corners. This increased his _____ even more. Today, jeans are as _____ as ever. All types of people, including _____ , _____ , and even _____ , can be seen wearing Levi jeans.

Organizing Information

Here is a list of important events in Levi Strauss's life. Put them in correct time order by numbering them from 1 to 7.

_____ **a.** Levi sold his first pair of pants.

_____ **b.** Levi left Germany to join his brothers in New York.

_____ **c.** He got a patent for riveted pockets.

_____ **d.** He moved to San Francisco.

_____ **e.** He began using blue denim to make his pants.

_____ **f.** Levi Strauss & Company was established.

_____ **g.** He left his business to his sister's children.

Figure it Out

Vocabulary in Context

Without using your dictionary, write an approximate definition or a synonym for the highlighted words in the following sentences. Then compare your answers with those of your classmates.

1. The Gold Rush, started in 1848, still **drew** men by the thousands to seek their fortunes.

_____

_____

2. Pleased with [his pants], his customer later **strutted** around San Francisco.

_____

_____

3. The demand for "Levi's" grew so fast that Strauss could hardly **keep up** with it.

_____

_____

4. When the brown canvas was gone, he **switched** to a sturdy fabric, _serge de Nîmes,_ from Nîmes, France.

_____

_____

5. Rivets strengthened the seams, which tore out when miners and other workers **stuffed** their pockets with gold nuggets and tools.

_____

_____

6. Davis was **flooded** with orders but worried that someone would steal his idea.

_____

_____

7. Today presidents, movie stars, and millions of other people wear Levis and other **brands** of jeans.

_____

_____

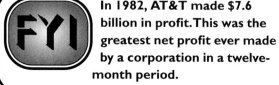

In 1982, AT&T made $7.6 billion in profit. This was the greatest net profit ever made by a corporation in a twelve-month period.

Talk it Over

Discussion Questions

1. Levi Strauss sold his first pair of pants in 1853. Today his idea for practical pants is still influencing the fashion world. Why do you think jeans are still so popular?

2. In the last paragraph the author states, "Levi Strauss found gold not in streams or mines, but in fulfilling an everyday need." What was the need that he fulfilled? What do you think made him such a successful entrepreneur? What are the qualities that make someone successful in business?

SELECTION 2

Our sense of smell can influence our behavior in many ways. Decisions about what we eat, what we wear, who we are attracted to, and even what we buy can be influenced by smell. In **Smells Sell!**, you will read about how advertisers use the sense of smell to increase sales.

Before You Read

Making Predictions

1. Read the title, subtitle, and headings of this article. Also, look at the picture. What do you think the article will be about? Write your prediction on the lines provided.

_____

_____

_____

2. Now read the first and last two paragraphs of the article. Can you make your prediction more specific?

_____

_____

_____

3. Finally, read the first sentence of each paragraph. Do you want to change your prediction at all? If so, write your new prediction below.

_____

_____

_____

Reading the Article

Now read the whole article, and do the exercises that follow.

Smells Sell!

MELINDA CROW

Scent Experts Lead You by the Nose

1 You're standing in the cereal aisle at the grocery store, searching for your favorite brand. Suddenly, you catch a whiff of chocolate-chip cookies. Your mouth begins to water. You forget about cereal and head for the bakery section.

2 Guess what? You just walked into a trap—an odor trap! The yummy smell was fake. The odor was cooked up by scientists in a lab, then spread by the store's owners to lure you to the bakery section.

DOLLARS AND SCENTS

3 For years, scientists have been studying the special powers of smells. It seems that our noses and our brains are very closely connected. When you smell something, the odor goes up your nose to smelling zones. From here, sense cells send nerve messages to your brain telling it what you smelled.

4 More than our other four senses, our sense of smell changes our mood and helps us remember things. If you were told to think about popcorn, you'd probably recall its smell. And then you might remember the movie you saw while eating it. Our sense of smell also helps us sniff out danger—like the smell of smoke. And it can make your mouth water from just one whiff of food.

5 If smell is so powerful, say store owners, then maybe it can also sell products. So businesses have begun spending thousands of dollars to scent entire stores. Fake scents are being used to lead customers by the nose. These bogus odors help to get people inside and put them in the mood to buy. They even make customers remember the store later, so they'll come back for more.

6 Some business people predict that in 10 years, store smells will be as common as the soft music stores often play to put shoppers in a good mood.

HIDDEN PELLETS AND GOO

7 J'Amy Owens designs stores for a living. To keep up with the new trend in store odors, she recently began including "fragrance planning" as part of her store design. She believes each store should have its own special smell.

8 For a kids' clothing store in San Francisco, CA, for example, she's using the smell of cinnamon and hot apple spice. She hopes shoppers will end up thinking these kids' clothes are as American as apple pie!

9 Sometimes Owens gets strange requests. "The owner of a fast-food restaurant wanted to know if I could scent the speaker at the drive-up window," she says.

10   Owens spreads the store scents secretly, using little balls soaked in fragrance. She hides them in light fixtures and heating pipes. If that doesn't give off enough odor, she puts in a small heater. This warms up the fragrance. A fan then spreads this smell throughout the store.

11   Other stores use computer-controlled machines to carry the smell out through the store's air vents. Getting the right amount of odor in the air can be tricky. When Steven Schultz first started using peach fragrance in his discount store in Louisville, KY, the whole place ended up smelling like a peach warehouse.

SOMETHING SMELLS FISHY

12   Dr. Alan Hirsch designs smells for businesses. He says that it doesn't take a whole lot of smell to affect you. Store owners can lure you to the candy aisle—even if you don't realize you're smelling candy. This idea scares a lot of people. Groups that protect the rights of shoppers are upset. They say the stores are using a kind of brainwashing, which they call "smellwashing."

13   "It's pretty sleazy," says Mark Silbergeld. He runs an organization that checks out products for consumers.

14   The scientists hired to design the scents disagree. "There's mellow background music, there's neon lighting, there are all sorts of bells and jingles being used," says Dr. Hirsch. "Why not smells?"

15   One reason why not, says Silbergeld, is that some people are allergic to certain scents pumped into products or stores.

16   But there's a whole other side to this debate. Do the smells really work? So far there is little proof one way or the other. But Dr. Hirsch has run some interesting experiments.

17   In one of Hirsch's experiments, 31 volunteers were led into a sneaker store that smelled slightly like flowers. Later, another group shopped in the same store, but with no flower odor.

18   Dr. Hirsch found that 84 percent of the shoppers were more likely to buy the sneakers in the flower-scented room. But Hirsch found out something even stranger.

19   "Whether the volunteers liked the flower scent or not didn't matter," Hirsch says. "Some reported that they hated the smell. But they still were more likely to buy the shoes in the scented room."

WHO KNOWS THE FUTURE?

20   Using smells to sell products isn't new. In 1966, a company added lemon fragrance to its dish detergent. They wanted people to think the soap contained "natural" cleaners. It worked! Today, businesses spend over a billion dollars a year just on product odor.

21   Some companies have already discovered ways to make microwaveable foods smell good before they're cooked. They scent the packages. Smell for yourself. Next time you pop a bag of microwave popcorn, smell the bag before you put it in the microwave. Chances are, it already smells like popped corn.

22   New uses for smells are being created every day. One bank, for example, gives customers coupons advertising car loans. To get people to take out a loan, bank officials hope to coat these coupons with the fresh leather smell of a new car.

23   In Australia, companies are putting sweat odor on unpaid bills. Since some people sweat when they're scared, this smell might remind them of when they are frightened. And they'll pay the bills right away.

24   What lies ahead for our noses? Smell scientists are working on some outrageous ideas. Would you believe TV sets that produce smells? Or how about odor diets? Certain food smells will fool your stomach into thinking it's full.

25   Alarm clocks will scent your bedroom with an aroma designed to wake you up. Scientists are even working on ways to keep garbage from stinking. And researchers expect scents to one day help students make more sense of what they're learning.

How Well Did You Read?

True/False

Read the statements that follow. If a statement is true, write T *on the line. If it is false, write* F.

_____ **1.** The sense of smell can change your mood and help you remember things.

_____ **2.** Because the sense of smell is so powerful, some businesses have begun using it to sell products.

_____ **3.** In the future, store smells might be as common as soft music.

_____ **4.** It takes a large amount of a certain smell to affect a customer.

_____ **5.** It is always easy to get the right amount of odor in the air.

_____ **6.** Some groups and organizations oppose the idea of using smells to attract and influence customers.

_____ **7.** There is a lot of evidence supporting the idea that smells influence customer behavior.

_____ **8.** Using smells to sell products is a new development in marketing.

_____ **9.** New uses for smells are being developed all the time.

Supporting Main Ideas

Using Examples

Find examples in the article to support each of the following ideas.

1. More than our other four senses, our sense of smell changes our mood and helps us remember things.

_____

_____

2. . . . each store should have its own special smell.

_____

_____

3. Getting the right amount of odor in the air can be tricky.

_____

_____

4. Using smells to sell products isn't new.

_____

_____

5. Some companies have already discovered ways to make microwaveable foods smell good before they're cooked.

_____

_____

6. New uses for smells are being created every day.

_____

_____

Building Vocabulary Skills

List all the words or phrases from the article that have to do with smell. Try to find as many as you can.

_____

_____

_____

_____

_____

_____

_____

_____

Figure It Out

Idioms And Expressions

An **idiom** is a phrase that has a special meaning. The meaning of the phrase as a whole is different from the meanings of the individual words in the phrase. For example, in the sentence, "I'm sure David was pulling my leg when he told me he had won the lottery," the idiom *pulling my leg* means teasing me.

An **expression** is also a group of words with a special meaning. For example, in the sentence, "She hopes shoppers will end up thinking these kids' clothes are as American as apple pie," the expression *as American as apple pie* means that something is very American.

"Smells Sell!" is filled with idioms and expressions. Circle the letter of the word or phrase that best describes the idiom.

1. You forget about cereal and **head for** the bakery section.
   a. walk toward
   b. point your head at
   c. remember

2. You just **walked into a trap**—an odor trap!
   a. avoided
   b. got tricked
   c. smelled

3. The odor was **cooked up** by scientists in a lab. . . .
   a. sold
   b. invented
   c. discussed

4. Fake scents are being used **to lead customers by the nose.**
   a. direct customers
   b. get rid of customers
   c. discourage customers

5. He runs an organization that **checks out** products for customers.
   a. removes
   b. leaves
   c. investigates

6. But Hirsch **found out** something even stranger.
   a. wrote about
   b. discovered
   c. examined

Talk it Over

Discussion Questions

1. Consider again how sensitive you are to smells. Do you think it's realistic to think that artificial smells can influence your buying behavior?

2. "Synthetic fragrances just add more chemicals to the chemical soup. It's an outrage." (Dr. Albert Robbins, environmental medicine specialist[1]) What do you think Dr. Robbins means? Do you think indoor air pollution is a major health risk?

3. Do you use incense, cologne, aftershave lotion, perfume, or potpourri? Which ones? Do you use them often?

SELECTION 3

The next reading is a book review called **The Gender-Spender Gap.** The book reviewed is *Why Women Pay More.* The purpose of a book review is to give a critical analysis and summary of the book. If the review is positive, it may make people want to buy the book.

Before You Read

Prereading Activity

1. Before you read the book review, discuss these words and expressions with your teacher and classmates.

bargain, bargaining	surcharge
discrepancy	sticker price
negotiate	trends
savvy	perils
abuses	scams
fraud	outrages

2. Look at the cover of *Why Women Pay More.* What technique does the author use to get you interested in reading the book?

_____

_____

_____

_____

[1] *The Environmental Magazine* (July/August 1993), 10.

First Reading

Skimming

Read the book review one time quickly and identify the statement that best expresses the main idea of Why Women Pay More.

1. *Why Women Pay More* compares the salaries of men and women and provides research showing that women usually make less money.

2. *Why Women Pay More* examines the process of buying a new car and offers some ways to make it easier.

3. *Why Women Pay More* discusses situations where women pay more than men for the same things and suggests ways women can get more for their money.

The Gender-Spender Gap

PETER NYE

1   Women pay more—and get less—than men for car insurance, haircuts, dry cleaning, and surgical operations. In *Why Women Pay More*, Frances Cerra Whittelsey, a veteran consumer affairs reporter who spent 15 years with *The New York Times* and *Newsday*, surveys a number of important consumer areas and suggests how women can get more for their money.

2   She points out that women buy about half the cars sold each year, yet pay more than men. White women pay $150 more for the identical car than a white man after they both went through a rehearsed process of bargaining. African-American men paid $400 more, and African-American women suffered the most—they were offered a price averaging $800 higher than white men.

3   "Furthermore, certain industries have simply charged us more for items and services identical to those provided to men," Whittelsey says. For example, women pay a surcharge for clothes alterations, which typically are included when men buy suits. "These 'traditional' pricing practices have been going on for so long, in fact, that most women have never even noticed the discrepancy."

4   As if these problems aren't enough, women often are paid 60 to 75 percent of what men earn for the same job. Whittelsey cites a study that shows women earn an average of 74 cents for every dollar that men are paid.

5   Women are also less likely than men to realize that a car sticker price is negotiable, she suggests. "The same may be true for other items like computers, telephone systems, appliances, home improvements, TVs and stereos—the list goes on and on," she writes. To avoid marketplace perils, she encourages women to negotiate for products and services.

The Gender-Spender Gap by Peter Nye. Adapted from "Book Review: The Gender-Spender Gap," published in *Public Citizen* Magazine, Sept./Oct. 1993. Reprinted with the permission of Peter Nye, editor *Public Citizen* Magazine.

Second Reading

Read the review of Why Women Pay More *again more carefully. Try not to use your dictionary, and don't worry if you can't understand every word.*

How Well Did You Read?

Answer the following questions.

1. What example does the author give to show that some industries charge women more than men for services?

   _____

   _____

   _____

2. How does the author of the book support her claim that women are often paid less than men for the same job?

   _____

   _____

   _____

   _____

3. In addition to cars, what other products may have prices that can be negotiated? Find several examples from the review.

   _____

   _____

   _____

   _____

4. Do you think this is a positive or negative review of the book? Why? Give specific examples from the review to support your answer.

   _____

   _____

   _____

   _____

UNIT 3

The World of Marketing

The presence of marketing can be felt in every field of business activity. Marketing includes everything that goes into researching, pricing, promoting, and distributing goods and services. Whenever you buy something, half of the money you spend goes to cover the cost of marketing. Marketing is important because it affects many aspects of your life. For example, the goods and services you buy, the stores you shop in, and the TV programs paid for by advertising are all available as a result of marketing efforts.

Points to Ponder

Discussion Questions

Think about and then discuss the following questions.

1. Make a list of some of your recent purchases. What kinds of things influenced your purchasing decisions? What are some factors you take into account when you buy something?

_____

_____

_____

_____

_____

2. In your opinion, is there a relationship between psychology and sales? If so, what is it?

3. Do you think there is a strong connection between culture and business? If so, how can this affect the way companies do business internationally? What kinds of cross-cultural problems might a company encounter when it does business in another country?

SELECTION 1

Advertisers have many different ways of promoting and selling their products. In **How to Analyze an Ad**, you will learn how to become a smarter consumer.

Before You Read

Prereading Questions

1. What kinds of ads do you like? Describe them and give some examples. What kinds of ads do you dislike? Why?

2. How are your purchasing decisions influenced by the ads you see, hear, or read?

3. Do you consider yourself to be an astute consumer? Why or why not?

How to Analyze an Ad

Advertisers use all kinds of strategies to get your attention and your dollars. By asking some basic questions, you can learn to cut through the hype.

By Phil Sudo

1 No one likes to be a sucker. If you don't pay attention, though, ads can make you one. You can protect yourself by learning how to analyze ads. Once you understand the strategies and techniques advertisers use—the buttons they're trying to push—you can spot attempts at manipulation and make better, more critical decisions about

what's being advertised. You can even heighten your appreciation of ads—which ones you think are good and which ones you think are bad.

2   So the next time you notice an ad, ask yourself some of these questions:

What Kind of Ad Is It?

3   The majority of ads are called *product ads*—those intended to promote the millions of different goods and services for sale, from baking soda to banking. Other kinds of ads include: *corporate ads,* which promote a company's image or philosophy rather than a product; *political ads,* which aim to generate votes for a candidate or against an opponent; and *public-service ads,* which offer help, promote a cause, or seek donations.

What's the Target?

4   One reason we ignore so many ads is because they're not aimed at us. Advertisers seek to maximize an ad's effectiveness by identifying a *target market*—the audience they most want to reach. To do so, they divide the market into categories: by age, sex, income level, education, geographic region, ethnic background, political leaning, life-style—the list goes on and on. A maker of hockey sticks, for example, is going to target young males who live in cold-weather areas and take part in sports. Thus, its hockey-stick ads would be tailored to appeal to the likes and desires of that market alone.

5   A company with a wide target audience, like McDonald's, will develop several different ads, each aimed at a specific segment of the market—one for teenagers, one in Spanish, one for black families. It may cost more than having a single ad designed for everybody, but it is a more calculated, direct method of selling.

Where Is the Ad Found?

6   It makes no sense for the seller of arthritis medication to run an ad on MTV, or for a skateboard maker to advertise on *Oprah.* Advertisers seek to place their ads in media viewed by their target audience. A public-safety department, for example, might put a billboard about seat belts near a site where accidents are high. Similarly, a ritzy mail-order house might send its catalogues only to ZIP codes like 90210 and other high-income areas.

What Is the Sales Pitch?

7   The foundation of an ad is the sales pitch. To make the pitch, ads play on our needs and desires—those basic, often instinctive forces that motivate us to do something. Says one corporate marketing director, "Fear, envy, vanity, health, utility, profit, pride, love, and entertainment. If you ever spend money, it will be for one of those reasons." Here is where your guard should go up. If you can identify the buttons an ad is trying to push, you can avoid manipulation.

What Is the Subtext?

8   All ads have a *subtext*—that is, a meaning beneath the surface. The subtext of an ad is often what causes the most controversy, usually for fostering sexism or racial and ethnic stereotypes. Ads for laundry detergent, for example, are sometimes criticized for portraying women only as housewives.

9   By looking at the deeper level of ads, you can critique not only the attitudes of the advertiser, but our culture at large—what we value, how we see ourselves. With that knowledge, you can buy into those values or not. At least you'll know you're not getting suckered.

Ad It Up, Break It Down

How savvy are you when it comes to looking at ads? Here are three magazine ads for you to analyze. Look at each one, then read the text that accompanies it. When you're done, use the questions at the end for classroom discussion. What other insights can you bring to these ads?

DIESEL JEANS IN *SPIN* MAGAZINE

What it says: "How to teach your children to love and care. Modern children need to solve their own problems: teaching kids to kill helps them deal directly with reality—but they learn so much quicker when you give them a guiding hand! Make them proud and confident! Man, if they never learn to blast the brains out of their neighbors what kind of damn future has this country of ours got???"

What it means: As urban kids have increasingly turned to guns to be cool, so have advertisers. Many teen-oriented ads today feature firearms, alarming critics who see it as glorifying guns and violence. This ad tries to have it both ways—visually showing a "cool guy" with a gun, then using the text to make fun of violence in society. The woman in the ad could be a target, or the "modern child" referred to in the text.

What do you think? What's the target market for this ad? What links does it make between guns and fashion? Do ads like this contribute to violence in society, or defuse it? How does it portray women?

ESPRIT JUNIOR SPORTSWEAR IN *SASSY* AND *GLAMOUR*

What it says: "Esprit" over a model's flower-painted face.

What it means: This ad assumes familiarity with the Esprit brand name, because it doesn't show any products. According to Esprit officials, the face paint is a reference to the "flower power" era of the 1970s, which the company's new clothing styles are emphasizing.

The ad is notable for using a black model. Although the appearance of black and ethnic models is on the rise in mainstream magazines, few have been signed to lucrative contracts with cosmetics companies. Most companies still favor white models because their target market is white. Critics say that over the years, advertisers have created a mainstream ideal of beauty that is white, subtly telling minorities that they don't meet the standard.

What do you think? What's the target market for this ad? How is the ad supposed to help Esprit's sales? Does the model's skin color affect how you view the ad? What effect do ads have on society's notions of beauty?

BARI-JAY DRESSES IN *YM* (FORMERLY *YOUNG MISS*)

What it says: "Supermodel prom," the opening page of a five-page photo spread on what to wear to the prom.

What it means: Technically, this is not an advertisement. According to *YM*, advertisers don't pay to have their merchandise featured in photo layouts. (Some publications solicit ads by promising feature articles if companies will buy ad space.) But in the corner text, the magazine lists the brand of the products, the prices, and where to buy them. And it describes the dress as something to "blow the competition off the dance floor." Some people believe fashion layouts like these blur the line between advertising and editorial opinion.

What do you think? What is the difference between this article and an ad? Does this article have more credibility than an ad? Would you, as an advertiser, threaten to pull your ads to pressure an editor's decision? Would you, as an editor, ever write something critical about a product made by one of your advertisers?

Expanding Vocabulary

Defining Terms

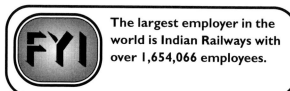
It is important to be able to recognize when a term is defined in the text. Sometimes an author will explain a word by putting the definition in parentheses, after a dash, or in a relative clause. Find the following words in the article and write a definition for each one.

1. product ads (¶3) _____

_____

_____

2. corporate ads (¶3) _____

_____

_____

3. political ads (¶3) _____

_____

_____

4. public-service ads (¶3) _____

_____

_____

5. target market (¶4) _____

_____

_____

6. sales pitch (¶7) _____

_____

_____

7. subtext (¶8) _____

_____

_____

Building Reading Skills

Making Inferences

*An **inference** is a reasonable conclusion that we make based on information that we have. It is an educated guess. Good readers are constantly making inferences based on the information provided in the text.*

Read the following statements. Put a check mark next to the statements you can infer from information in the article.

_____ **1.** By learning how to analyze ads, you can avoid being a sucker.

_____ **2.** Advertisers try to manipulate your decisions.

_____ **3.** There are fewer political ads than corporate ads.

_____ **4.** Coca Cola has different ads aimed at different segments of the market.

_____ **5.** It is possible to learn something about the values of a culture from its ads.

_____ **6.** MTV is not a good place to run ads for older people.

_____ **7.** Advertisers can use zip codes to identify certain types of target markets.

_____ **8.** Most people who eat at McDonald's are teenagers.

Application of Information

Analyzing Subtexts

1. According to the author, the subtext of many ads can be controversial. Some ads seem to promote sexism and racism. Others encourage ethnic stereotyping. Look through some magazines for ads with controversial subtexts. Cut them out and bring them to class. Be prepared to explain the subtexts of the ads and what they show.

2. The subtext of an ad can also give clues about the values of a culture. Some American values that ads try to show include the importance of family life, planning for the future, hard work, looking young, cleanliness, and getting your money's worth. Look for ads that express some of these values and bring them to class.

3. Choose one of the following topics and prepare a short presentation.
   a. Advertisements are a reflection of society.
   b. Advertisements are a powerful tool that can change society.
   c. Advertising in the United States is different from advertising in my native country.
   d. We are manipulated by advertisements.

SELECTION 2

The following two articles deal with various aspects of international business. The first one, **Do's and Taboos: Cultural Aspects of International Business**, focuses on cultural differences that can affect all areas of international business practices and decisions. The second article, **Big Blunders from Big Business**, deals more specifically with the marketing and advertising problems that can arise when companies try to sell their products abroad.

Before You Read

1. A **taboo** is something that is forbidden according to custom. Discuss the concept of taboos in your culture. What examples of taboos you can think of?

2. Look through the article and read the five callouts in bold print in the margin. From these, make some predictions about the kinds of things the author might discuss in the article.

_____

_____

_____

_____

Do's and Taboos

Cultural Aspects of International Business

BY M. KATHERINE GLOVER

Writer, Business America
International Trade Administration

1   Never touch the head of a Thai or pass an object over it, as the head is considered sacred in Thailand. Likewise, never point the bottoms of the feet in the direction of another person in Thailand or cross your legs while sitting, especially in the presence of an older person.

2   Avoid using triangular shapes in Hong Kong, Korea, or Taiwan, as the triangle is considered a negative shape in those countries.

3   Remember that the number 7 is considered bad luck in Kenya, good luck in Czechoslovakia, and has magical connotations in Benin.

4   Red is a positive color in Denmark, but represents witchcraft and death in many African countries.

5   A nod means "no" in Bulgaria, and shaking the head side-to-side means "yes."

6   Understanding and heeding cultural variables such as these is one of the most significant aspects of being successful in any international business endeavor. A lack of familiarity with the business practices, social customs, and etiquette of a country can weaken a company's position in the market, prevent it from accomplishing its objectives, and ultimately lead to failure.

7   As business has become increasingly international and communications technology continues to develop, the need for clearly understood communication between members of different cultures is even more crucial.

8   Growing competition for international markets is another reason that companies must consider cultural distinctions. As Secretary of Commerce Robert Mosbacher indicated, "American companies have to rely on all available tactics for winning in the global marketplace today. Learning international business diplomacy should be the first step they take."

Do's and Taboos: Cultural Aspects of International Business by M. Katherine Glover. Published in *Business America*, August 13, 1990, pp. 2–6. Reprinted with the permission of *Business America.*

9   Business executives who are not alert to cultural differences simply cannot function efficiently overseas. They may not even understand something as basic as what signifies closing a deal in a particular country—a handshake, a written contract, or a memorandum of understanding.

10   Taking the time to learn something about the culture of a country before doing business there is also a show of respect and is usually deeply appreciated, not to mention rewarding for the company. Those who understand the culture are more likely to develop successful, long-term business relationships.

11   Customs vary widely from one country to another. Something with one meaning in one area may mean the opposite somewhere else. Some of the cultural distinctions that firms most often face include differences in business styles, attitudes towards development of business relationships, attitudes towards punctuality, negotiating styles, gift-giving customs, greetings, significance of gestures, meanings of colors and numbers, and customs regarding titles.

> **Adapting to culture variables is a significant part of any international business endeavor.**

12   American firms must pay close attention to different styles of doing business and the degree of importance placed on developing business relationships. In some countries, business people have a very direct style, while in others they are much more subtle in style. Many nationalities value the personal relationship more than most Americans do in business. In these countries, long-term relationships based on trust are necessary for doing business. Many U.S. firms make the mistake of rushing into business discussions and "coming on too strong" instead of nurturing the relationship first. According to Roger Axtell in his book *Do's and Taboos of Hosting International Visitors,* "There is much more to business than just business in many parts of the world. Socializing, friendships, etiquette, grace, patience, and protocol are integral parts of business. Jumping right into business discussions before a get-acquainted interlude can be a bad mistake."

13   Charles Ford, Commercial Attaché in Guatemala, cites this cultural distinction as the greatest area of difference between the American and Guatemalan styles of doing business. The inexperienced American visitor, he claims, often tries to force a business relationship. The abrupt "always watching the clock" style rarely works in Guatemala. A better informed business executive would, he advises, engage in small talk about Guatemala, indicate an interest in the families of his or her business associates, join them for lunch or dinner, and generally allow time for a personal relationship to develop. Solid business opportunities usually follow a strong personal relationship in Guatemala. This holds true for Latin America in general.

14   Building a personal rapport is also important when doing business in Greece, according to Sondra Snowdon, President of Snowdon's International Protocol, Inc., a firm that trains and prepares executives in cross-cultural communications. Business entertaining is usually done in the evening at a local taverna, and spouses are often included. The relaxed atmosphere is important to building a business relationship based on friendship.

15   Belgians, however, are the opposite, Snowdon says. They are likely to get down to business right away and are unusually conservative and efficient in their approach to business meetings.

16   Attitudes toward punctuality vary greatly from one culture to another and unless understood can cause confusion and misunderstanding. Romanians, Japanese, and Germans are very punctual, while many of the Latin countries have a more relaxed attitude toward time. The Japanese consider it rude to be late for a business meeting, but it is acceptable, even fashionable, to be late for a social occasion.

> **Learning about a country's culture is a show of respect and is always appreciated.**

17   In Guatemala on the other hand, according to Ford, a luncheon at a specified time means that some guests might be 10 minutes early, while others may be 45 minutes late.

18   When crossing cultural lines, something as simple as a greeting can be misunderstood. The form of greeting differs from culture to culture. Traditional greetings may be a handshake, hug, nose rub, kiss, placing the hands in praying position, or various other gestures. Lack of awareness concerning the country's accepted form of greeting can lead to awkward encounters.

19   The Japanese bow is one of the most well-known forms of greeting. The bow symbolizes respect and humility and is a very important custom to observe when doing business with the Japanese. There are also different levels of bowing,

each with a significant meaning. Japanese and Americans often combine a handshake with a bow so that each culture may show the other respect.

20   Handshakes are the accepted form of greeting in Italy. Italians use a handshake for greetings and goodbyes. Unlike the United States, men do not stand when a woman enters or leaves a room, and they do not kiss a woman's hand. The latter is reserved for royalty.

21   The traditional Thai greeting, the wai, is made by placing both hands together in a prayer position at the chin and bowing slightly. The higher the hands, the more respect is symbolized. The fingertips should never be raised above eye level. The gesture means "thank you" and "I'm sorry" as well as "hello." Failure to return a wai greeting is equivalent to refusing to shake hands in the West.

22   According to Snowdon, American intentions are often misunderstood and Americans are sometimes perceived as not meaning what they say. For example, in Denmark the standard American greeting "Hi, how are you?" leads the Danes to think the U.S. business person really wants to know how they are. She suggests that, "Hi, I'm pleased to meet you" is preferable and conveys a more sincere message.

The traditional Thai greeting, the wai.

When crossing cultural lines something as simple as a greeting can be misunderstood.

23   People around the world use body movements or gestures to convey specific messages. Though countries sometimes use the same gestures, they often have very different meanings. Misunderstandings over gestures is a common occurrence in cross-cultural communication, and misinterpretation along these lines can lead to business complications and social embarrassment.

24   The "OK" sign commonly used in the United States is a good example of a gesture that has several different meanings according to the country. In France, it means zero; in Japan, it is a symbol for money; and in Brazil, it carries a vulgar connotation.

25   Assistant Commercial Attaché in the United Kingdom Thomas Kelsey advises that American businessmen should never sit with the ankle resting on the knee. They should instead cross their legs with one knee on top of the other. He also suggests avoiding backslapping and putting an arm around a new acquaintance.

26   In Thailand, it is considered offensive to place one's arm over the back of the chair in which another person is sitting, and men and women should not show affection in public.

27   The use of a palm-up hand and moving index finger signals "come here" in the United States and in some other countries but is considered vulgar in others. In Ethiopia, holding out the hand palm down and repeatedly closing the hand means "come here."

28   Proper use of names and titles is often a source of confusion in international business relations. In many countries (including the United Kingdom, France, and Denmark), it is appropriate to use titles until use of first names is suggested.

29   First names are seldom used when doing business in Germany. Visiting business people should use the surname preceded by the title. Titles such as "Herr Direktor" are sometimes used to indicate prestige, status, and rank.

30   Thais, on the other hand, address each other by first names and reserve last names for very formal occasions, or in writing. When using the first name, they often use the honorific "Khun" or a title preceding it. In Belgium, it is important to address French-speaking business contacts as "Monsieur" or "Madame," while Dutch-speaking contacts should be addressed as "Mr." or "Mrs." According to Sondra Snowdon, to confuse the two is a great insult.

31   Customs concerning gift-giving are extremely important to understand. In some cultures, gifts are expected, and failure to present them is considered an insult, whereas in other countries, offering a gift is considered offensive. Business executives also need to know when to present gifts—on the initial visit or afterwards; where to present gifts—in public or private; what type of gift to present; what color it should be; and how many to present.

32   Gift-giving is an important part of doing business in Japan. Exchanging gifts symbolizes the depth and strength of a business relationship to the Japanese. Gifts are usually exchanged at the first meeting. When presented with a gift, companies are expected to respond by giving a gift.

33   In sharp contrast, gifts are rarely exchanged in Germany and are usually not appropriate. Small gifts are fine, but expensive items are not a general practice.

34   Gift-giving is not a normal custom in Belgium or the United Kingdom either, although in both countries, flowers are a suitable gift if invited to someone's home. Even that is not as easy as it sounds. International executives must use caution to choose appropriate flowers. For example, avoid sending chrysanthemums (especially white) in Belgium and elsewhere in Europe since they are mainly used for funerals. In Europe, it is also considered bad luck to present an even number of flowers. Beware of white flowers in Japan where they are associated with death, and purple flowers in Mexico and Brazil.

> **Americans have not had a good track record of being sensitive to cultural distinctions.**

35   Yue-Sai Kan, host and executive producer of a television show about Asia—*Looking East*—and of a new four-part series on *Doing Business in Asia,* points out that customs toward the exchange of business cards vary, too. Seemingly minor in importance, observance of a country's customs towards card-giving is a key part of business protocol.

36   In Japan, it is particularly important to be aware of the way business cards should be exchanged, according to Yue-Sai Kan. The western tradition of accepting a business card and immediately putting it in your pocket is considered very rude there, she contends. The proper approach is to carefully look at the card after accepting it, observe the title and organization, acknowledge with a nod that you have digested the information, and perhaps make a relevant comment or ask a polite question. During a meeting, spread the cards in front of you relating to where people are sitting. In other words says Yue-Sai Kan, treat a business card as you would treat its owner—with respect.

37   When presenting a card in either Japan or South Korea, it is important to use both hands and position the card so that the recipient can read it. In any country where English is not commonly taught, the data should be printed in the native language on the reverse side of the card.

38   Negotiating can be a complex process between parties from the same nation. Negotiating across cultures is even more complicated because of the added chance of misunderstanding stemming from cultural differences. Negotiating styles differ from nation to nation. In addition, a host of cultural variables must be dealt with all at once.

39   For example, it is essential to understand the importance of rank in the other country and to know who the decision makers are. It is equally important to be familiar with the business style of the foreign company. Is it important to be direct or subtle? Is it necessary to have an established relationship with the company before beginning negotiations? Executives negotiating with foreign companies must also understand the nature of agreements in the country, the significance of gestures, and negotiating etiquette.

40   These cultural variables are examples of the things that U.S. executives involved in international business must be aware of. At times in the past, Americans have not had a good track record of being sensitive to cultural distinctions. However, as business has become more global, Americans have become more sensitive to cultural differences and the importance of dealing with them effectively. Still, some companies fail to do their homework and make fatal or near-fatal mistakes that could have easily been prevented. A number of firms have learned the hard way that successful domestic strategies do not necessarily work overseas and that business must be adapted to the culture.

> **Failure to research and understand a culture has led to many international business blunders.**

41   Failure to research and understand a culture before entering the market has led to many international business blunders. They run the gamut from forgivable to disastrous. Some years ago, for example, a leading U.S. golf ball manufacturer targeted Japan as an important new market for golf. However, sales of the company's golf balls were well below average. The firm, as it turned out, had packaged the balls in groups of four—the number of death in Japan.

42   David Ricks, in his book *Big Business Blunders: Mistakes in Multinational Marketing,* cites a number of other blunders that resulted from cultural oversights. One concerns a telephone company that tried to incorporate a Latin

flavor in its commercial by employing Puerto Rican actors. In the ad, the wife said to her husband, "Run downstairs and phone Mary. Tell her we'll be a little late." The commercial contained two major cultural errors: Latin wives seldom dare order their husbands around, and almost no Latin would feel it necessary to phone to warn of tardiness since it is expected.

43 Another company experienced headaches caused by poor translation. A Mexican magazine promotion for an American-brand shirt carried a message stating the opposite of what had originally been intended. The advertisement, instead of reading "when I used this shirt, I felt good," said "until I used this shirt, I felt good."

44 A toothpaste company tried to sell its product in regions of Southeast Asia through a promotion which stressed that the toothpaste helped enhance white teeth. In this area, where some local people deliberately chewed betel nut in order to achieve the social prestige of darkly stained teeth, such an ad was less than effective. The slogan "wonder where the yellow went" was also viewed as a racial slur.

45 Mistakes of these types can at the least reduce sales, and at the worst, give the company and the product such a bad name that it closes out the market entirely. To avoid blunders like this, a company ultimately must not only have a sensitivity to other cultures but also must have a good understanding of its own culture and how other countries see American culture.

Building Reading Skills

Scanning For Supporting Examples

Scanning is a quick way to locate specific information in a passage. Scanning is different from reading. When you scan, you move your eyes very quickly across and down the page with one purpose: to find the information you need.

Scan the article to find specific examples to support the following generalizations. Complete the chart below.

Numbers have different meanings around the world.
Colors have different connotations in different countries.
Shapes do not always mean the same thing everywhere.
The style of doing business varies from country to country.
Attitudes toward punctuality differ from one place to another.

Even something as simple as a greeting can be misunderstood.
People around the world use different gestures and body movements to convey specific meanings.
Proper use of names and titles is often a source of confusion in international business relations.
Gift-giving customs in other countries require careful attention.

Expanding Vocabulary

Synonyms or Antonyms

Decide if the following pairs of words are synonyms or antonyms. If they are synonyms, circle S. If they are antonyms, circle A.

1.	connotation	implication	S	A
2.	subtle	direct	S	A
3.	crucial	unimportant	S	A
4.	abrupt	gradual	S	A
5.	punctual	late	S	A
6.	etiquette	protocol	S	A
7.	suitable	appropriate	S	A
8.	contend	claim	S	A
9.	incorporate	exclude	S	A
10.	deliberately	intentionally	S	A

Expanding Vocabulary

Defining Terms

Choose five words from this article that are new to you and teach them to your classmates. Present a definition for each word and a sentence that uses the word.

1. _____

_____

2. _____

_____

3. _____

_____

4. _____

_____

5. _____

TYING IT ALL TOGETHER

Word Forms

A. *Complete the chart by filling in the missing forms of the words. The verb forms have been given.*

Verb	Noun	Adjective	Adverb
appreciate			
collaborate			
distinguish			
manipulate			
negotiate			
persuade			
promote			
rationalize			
recognize			
signify			

B. *Correct the sentences that have errors in word forms.*

1. After many years of <u>collaboratively</u>, the authors finally finished the book.

2. My cousin had lost so much weight that I didn't <u>recognition</u> him.

3. Advertisers hope that their campaigns are <u>persuasively</u> enough to attract many buyers.

4. I'm too tired to make a <u>rationalize</u> decision right now.

5. Customers <u>appreciative</u> helpful sales people.

6. The oil industry is of great <u>signify</u> to our economy.

7. After many meetings, the union finally <u>negotiable</u> a new contract with management.

8. It is difficult to work for Kris because she is a very <u>manipulatively</u> manager.

9. It is often difficult to <u>distinguished</u> subtle differences between cultures.

10. The car company's sales <u>promotional</u> was very successful.

SELECTION 3

The first rule of advertising is know your target market. This is especially true in today's global marketplace where cultural differences come into play. In **Big Blunders from Big Business**, you will read about several instances in which marketers failed to follow that rule and the sometimes humorous, but always costly, consequences.

Big Blunders from Big Business

Mistakes in Global Marketing Can be Embarassing and Costly

1 International marketing can be a tricky business. With the increase in global trade, international companies cannot afford to make costly advertising mistakes if they want to be competitive and profitable. Understanding the language and culture of target markets in foreign countries is one of the keys to successful international marketing. Too many companies, however, have jumped into foreign markets with embarrassing results. Out of their blunders, a whole new industry of translation services has emerged.

FAULTY TRANSLATIONS

2 The value of understanding the language of a country cannot be overestimated. Translation mistakes are at the heart of many blunders in international advertising. Since a language is more than the sum of its words, a literal, word-by-word dictionary translation seldom works. The following examples prove this point. Otis Engineering Company once displayed a poster at a trade show in Moscow that turned heads. Due to a poor translation of its message, the sign boasted that the firm's equipment was great for improving a person's sex life. The Parker Pen Company suffered an embarrassing moment when it realized that a faulty translation of one of its ads into Spanish resulted in a promise to "help prevent unwanted pregnancies."

3 Automobile manufacturers in the United States have made several notorious advertising mistakes that have been well publicized. General Motors learned a costly lesson when it introduced its Chevrolet Nova to the Puerto Rican market. Although "nova" means "star" in Spanish, when it is spoken, it sounds like "no va" which means "it doesn't

go." Few people wanted to buy a car with that meaning. When GM changed the name to Caribe, sales picked up dramatically. Ford also ran into trouble with the name of one of its products. When it introduced a low-cost truck called the "Fiera" into Spanish-speaking countries, Ford didn't realize until too late that the name meant "ugly old woman" in Spanish. Another American auto manufacturer made a mistake when it translated its Venezuelan ad for a car battery. It was no surprise when Venezuelan customers didn't want to buy a battery that was advertised as being "highly overrated."

Ads for American products can show up in the most unlikely places, like this little café in a remote Moroccan village.

4   Airline companies have also experienced problems of poor translation. A word-by-word translation ruined a whole advertising campaign for Braniff Airlines. Hoping to promote its plush leather seats, Braniff's ad urged passengers to "fly on leather." However, when the slogan was translated into Spanish, it told customers to "fly naked." Another airline company, Eastern Airlines, made a similar mistake when it translated its motto, "We earn our wings daily" into Spanish. The poor translation suggested that its passengers often ended up dead.

5   Marketing blunders have also been made by food and beverage companies. One American food company's friendly "Jolly Green Giant" became something quite different when it was translated into Arabic as "Intimidating Green Ogre." When translated into German, Pepsi's popular slogan, "Come Alive with Pepsi" came out implying "Come Alive from the Grave." No wonder customers in Germany didn't rush out to buy Pepsi. Even a company with an excellent international track record like Kentucky Fried Chicken is not immune to the perils of faulty translation. A lot of sales were lost when the catch phrase "finger lickin' good" became "eat your fingers off" in the Chinese translation.

6   A manufacturer of one laundry detergent made an expensive mistake in a promotional campaign in the Middle East. The advertisements showed a picture of a pile of dirty clothes on the left, a box of the company's detergent in the middle, and clean clothes on the right. Unfortunately, the message was incorrectly interpreted because most people in the Middle East read from right to left. It seemed to them that the detergent turned clean clothes into dirty ones.

CULTURAL OVERSIGHTS CAN BE DISASTROUS

7   Successful international marketing doesn't stop with good translations—other aspects of culture must be researched and understood if marketers are to avoid blunders. When marketers do not understand and appreciate the values, tastes, geography, climate, superstitions, level of literacy, religion, or economic development of a culture, they fail to capture their target market. For example, when a popular American designer tried to introduce a new perfume in the Latin American market, the product aroused little interest and the company lost a lot of money. Ads for the new fragrance highlighted its fresh camellia scent. What marketers had failed to realize was that camellias are traditionally used for funerals in many South American countries.

8   Procter and Gamble has been successful in marketing its products internationally for many years. Today, overseas markets account for over one third of its sales. However, the company's success in this area didn't happen overnight. Procter and Gamble initially experienced huge losses because marketing managers did not recognize important cultural differences. For instance, when P&G first entered the Japanese market with its popular Cheer laundry detergent, most Japanese housewives weren't interested. The promotional campaign that emphasized Cheer as an effective "all temperature" detergent was lost on the Japanese who usually wash clothes in cold water.

Although the pitch had been quite successful in the United States where clothes are washed in all temperatures, it fell flat in Japan. All of this could have been avoided if P&G marketers had done more preliminary research before launching the campaign. Once P&G changed its strategy and promised superior cleaning in cold water, sales for Cheer picked up dramatically.

9   The use of numbers can also be a source of problems for international marketers. Since every culture has its own set of lucky and unlucky numbers, companies need to do their homework if they want to avoid marketing blunders. A U.S. manufacturer of golf balls learned this lesson the hard way when it packaged its product in groups of four for export to Japan. The company couldn't figure out why the golf balls weren't selling well until it realized that in Japanese the word for the number four also means death. In Japan four and nine are very unlucky numbers which should be avoided by marketers.

10 Even illustrations need to be carefully examined. A picture that is culturally offensive can ruin an advertisement even if the written message is properly translated. McDonnell Douglas Corporation made an unfortunate error in an aircraft brochure for potential customers in India. It included a picture of men wearing turbans, which was not appreciated by the Indians. A company spokesman reported, "It was politely pointed out to us that turbans were distinctly Pakistani Moslem." The artist for the ad had used an old National Geographic magazine to copy the picture.

PREVENTING BLUNDERS

11 Having awakened to the special nature of foreign advertising, companies are becoming much more conscientious in securing accurate translations. They are also becoming much more sensitive to the cultural distinctions and variables that play such an important role in any international business venture. Above all, the best way to guard against errors is to hire trained professional translators who thoroughly understand the target language and its idiomatic usage. These translators should be very familiar with the culture and people of the country, and have a grasp of the technical aspects of the industry.

12 Many international companies are using a technique called "backtranslation," which greatly reduces the possibility of advertising blunders. The process of backtranslation requires one person to translate the message into the target language and another person to translate the new version back into the original language. The purpose is to determine whether the original material and the retranslated material are the same. In this way companies can ensure that their intended message is really being conveyed.

13 Effective translators aim to capture the overall message of an advertisement because a word-for-word duplication of the original rarely conveys the intended meaning and often causes misunderstandings. In designing advertisements to be used in other countries, marketers are recognizing the need to keep messages as short and simple as possible and to avoid idioms, jargon, and slang that are difficult to translate. Similarly, they avoid jokes, since humor does not translate well from one culture to another. What is considered funny in one part of the world may not be so humorous in another. The bottom line is that consumers interpret advertising in terms of their own cultures. As the global marketplace opens up, there is no room for linguistic or cultural blunders.

How Well Did You Read?

In small groups, identify the reasons that each of the following advertising campaigns failed.

1. General Motor's Chevrolet Nova in Puerto Rico

_____

_____

2. Braniff Airline's promotion for leather seats in Spanish-speaking countries

_____

_____

3. Kentucky Fried Chicken's advertisement in China

_____

_____

4. an American laundry detergent ad in the Middle East

_____

_____

5. an American designer's perfume campaign in South America

_____

_____

6. Procter and Gamble's ad for Cheer in Japan

_____

_____

7. an American company's packaging of golf balls for export to Japan

_____

_____

8. McDonnell Douglas Corporation's brochure for India

_____

_____

 The largest manufacturing company in the world is General Motors Company of Detroit, Michigan with operations throughout the world, 710,000 employees, and net sales of over $2 billion annually.

Figure it Out

Idioms

Using the context of the sentence, write a definition for the highlighted expressions.

1. Translation mistakes are **at the heart of** many blunders in international marketing.

   _____

2. Otis Engineering Company once displayed a poster at a trade show in Moscow that **turned heads.**

   _____

3. Ford also **ran into** trouble with the name of one of its products.

   _____

4. Even a company with an excellent international **track record** like Kentucky Fried Chicken is not immune to the perils of faulty translation.

   _____

5. A lot of sales were lost when the **catch phrase** "finger lickin' good" became "eat your fingers off" in Chinese.

   _____

6. The promotional campaign that emphasized Cheer as an effective "all temperature" detergent was **lost on** the Japanese who usually wash clothes in cold water.

   _____

7. Although the pitch had been quite successful in the United States where clothes are washed in all temperatures, it **fell flat** in Japan.

   _____

8. Once P&G changed its strategy and promised superior cleaning in cold water, sales for Cheer **picked up** dramatically.

   _____

9. **The bottom line** is that consumers interpret advertising in terms of their own cultures.

   _____

Talk it Over

Discussion Questions

Write five discussion questions for your classmates to answer based on issues raised in "Do's and Taboos" and "Big Blunders from Big Business." Then discuss the answers in small groups.

1. _____

2. _____

3. _____

4. _____

5. _____

WRITING SECTION

UNIT 4

Comparison-Contrast

PART 1: ORGANIZATION

Comparison-Contrast Essays

Comparing and contrasting, or thinking about similarities and differences, is an activity that we do every day whenever we have to make decisions. When buying a new car, you compare and contrast several cars before choosing one. When thinking about what classes to take next semester, you compare and contrast the teachers and the class hours before making your choices. Even deciding where to eat involves comparing and contrasting.

We also frequently make comparisons and contrasts in writing. In the business world, you may have to evaluate proposals from two companies who want to do business with you, or you may have to evaluate two job applicants, two computer systems, or two health insurance plans. This chapter will show you how to do this.

Block Organization

A comparison and contrast essay can be organized in several ways. However in this book, you will learn the most basic pattern, which is called **block organization.**

In block organization, the similarities are discussed together in one block (which can be one paragraph or several paragraphs). Then the differences are discussed together in one block. As you can see from this outline, the model essay uses block organization. The two paragraphs of similarities are a block, and the four paragraphs of differences are a block.

SCHOOL SYSTEMS IN EUROPE AND THE UNITED STATES

I. Introduction
   A. General statements
   B. Thesis statement

II. Similarities—elementary schools
    A. Class size and composition
    B. One teacher
    C. Curriculum

III. Similarities—years of compulsory education
     A. Number of years
     B. Ages

IV. Differences—schedule
    A. Hours per day
    B. Days per year

V. Differences in types of schools
   A. One sequence or two
   B. Academic and vocational

VI. Differences in private schools
    A. Religious and not religious
    B. Financing

VII. Differences—higher education

VIII. Conclusion
      A. Concluding sentence(s)
      B. Final thoughts

You may, of course, discuss the differences first and then the similarities.

Thesis Statements

The thesis statement in a comparison-contrast essay should clearly name the topics of the comparison. It should also indicate that this is going to be a comparison-contrast analysis. The thesis statement sometimes also names the points on which the topics are going to be compared and contrasted. Let's look at the thesis statement of the model essay.

ABOVE MATERIAL FROM: INTRODUCTION TO ACADEMIC WRITING

However, a comparison of school systems in Europe and the United States reveals several similarities but a great number of differences.

The topics are named:

school systems in Europe and school systems in the United States

These words show that the essay will be a comparison-contrast analysis:

a comparison of
several similarities but a great number of differences

Here are some further examples of thesis statements for comparison and contrast. These sentences are about two car models.

Comparison only: The Super XL and the Magna XL are alike in several ways.

Contrast only: The Super XL and the Magna XL have some very important differences.

Comparison and contrast: The Super XL and the Magna XL have both similarities and differences.

Contrast, with points named: The Super XL and the Magna XL are different in exterior design, interior design, and comfort.

Concluding Paragraphs

The concluding paragraph of a comparison- contrast essay can follow the same pattern as other conclusions: concluding sentence(s) followed by the writer's final thoughts. The concluding sentence of the model essay restates the thesis in different words:

Even though the countries of Europe and the United States seem very similar in many ways, their educational systems are quite different.

The final comment is often a recommendation or a judgment in a comparison-contrast essay:

For the same money, I believe the Magna XL is the better car to buy.
Based on these data, I recommend that our company buy the XYZ rather than the ABC computer system.

However, in the model essay, the writer wanted to avoid making a judgment:

No one can say if one system is better than another system, for each one fits its own needs, economies, and traditions the best.

Practice

Organizing a Comparison-Contrast Topic

Work with a partner or a small group. You are a travel agent, and a wealthy client has asked you to help her decide on a vacation destination. She wants to go during the summer, and she is considering Alaska and Hawaii. Both places are popular tourist destinations. You have gathered some information about the two places. You now need to organize this information and prepare a written report.

1. Study the list of information about Alaska and Hawaii. Clarify any unfamiliar vocabulary.
2. The information is not in any order. Organize the information by filling in the chart that follows. Begin by assigning the items to one of the following main topics:

> Accommodations (hotels and restaurants)
> Environment
> Transportation
> Climate
> Natural Beauty

Then put the information in the appropriate boxes.

> The ocean and rivers in Alaska are unpolluted.
> There is no air pollution in Hawaii.
> The temperature is perfect in Alaska during the summer.
> The food in Alaska is poor in quality and expensive.
> There is no humidity in Alaska.
> Alaska has the Chugach Mountains and Mount McKinley, the highest mountain in North America.
> There is a wide variety of excellent restaurants in Hawaii.
> It is terribly humid in Hawaii in the summer.
> Most people fly to Hawaii by jumbo jet.
> Hawaii has Volcano National Park and Waimea Canyon.
> It can be very hot in Hawaii in the summer.
> The ocean surrounding Hawaii is clean, and the rivers are unpolluted.

ABOVE MATERIAL FROM: INTRODUCTION TO ACADEMIC WRITING

The beaches in Hawaii are among the most beautiful in the world.

The glaciers in Alaska are awesome.

Hotels in Alaska are expensive, and their quality is generally poor.

The air in Alaska is pure and clean.

It often rains during the summer in Hawaii.

Most people travel to Alaska by cruise ship.

There is a wide range of excellent hotels in Hawaii, from luxury to budget priced.

It's impractical to rent a car in Alaska because the distances are too great.

Rental cars are cheap and convenient in Hawaii.

It seldom rains during the summer in Alaska.

	ALASKA	HAWAII
ACCOMMODATIONS		
ENVIRONMENT		
TRANSPORTATION		
CLIMATE		
NATURAL BEAUTY	Chugach Mountains and Mount McKinley	

3. Make a formal outline for your report. Your outline should have seven paragraphs. Include these in your outline:

A thesis statement

A conclusion (Make a recommendation to your client.)

Paragraphs of similarities

Paragraphs of differences

Topic sentences for each paragraph

Use the outline on page 58 as a model.

PART 2: SENTENCE STRUCTURE

MODEL ESSAY

Comparison-Contrast Structure Words

As you read the model essay, look for words and phrases that show similarities and differences.

GENDER[1] DIFFERENCES

The "battle of the sexes" started with Adam and Eve,[2] and it will probably continue forever. The opinion that men are superior to women has long been accepted in many cultures, but the feminist movement[3] is trying to change this view. Feminists claim that boys and girls are exactly equal at birth but become unequal because of the way they are treated by society. However, recent research contradicts[4] the view that males and females are innately[5] alike.

Without a doubt, societal influences both inside and outside the family cause many differences to develop. Inside the family, boys learn to be men by watching and copying their fathers, and girls learn to be women by watching and copying their mothers. Outside the family, boys who play with dolls after a certain age receive disapproval, as do girls who continue to play with Ninja Turtles (although the pressure may not be quite as strong on girls).

However, not all differences are caused by societal influences. Some are due to differences in the physiology[6] of the brain. For example, more men than women are left-handed, which means that the right side of men's brains are dominant[7] because the right side of the brain controls the left side of the body. Right-brain people generally have better reasoning abilities, whereas left-brain people generally have better verbal skills.

In fact, girls are better at language than boys. For both men and women, the language center is on the left side of the brain. However, girls not only begin speaking earlier than boys, but they also speak more clearly and develop larger vocabularies. In contrast, more boys than girls stutter[8] and have trouble learning to read. Boys' difficulty with language may be the result of their right-brain dominance.

In addition, men and women have different spatial abilities. For example, men are better at turning three-dimensional[9] objects in their heads. That's why they can read maps more easily than women. Women often have to turn a map around in order to know which direction to go, whereas men can do it in their heads. On the other hand, women excel at other spatial tasks such as remembering the location of objects in a random[10] pattern. That's why women are better than men at finding misplaced car keys and eyeglasses.

While it is clear that some differences are rooted in the physiology of the brain, it is equally clear that other differences are not. For example, boys and girls are equal in math ability until about seventh grade. Then girls start to fall behind, perhaps because math teachers encourage boys more. Furthermore, there are many exceptions to these general patterns. Just as some women are good at abstract algebra, some men become skilled poets and public speakers.

Although continuing research will yield further information about gender differences, it will never resolve[11] the battle between the sexes. However, it should help the next time **he** gets lost in the family car while following **her** map-reading directions, and the next time **she** has to look for **his** misplaced car keys.

---

[1]**gender:** sex; [2]**Adam and Eve:** the first man and woman, according to Judeo-Christian tradition; [3]**feminist movement:** activities and people in support of equality for women; [4]**contradicts:** says or proves that the opposite is true; [5]**innately:** by birth, naturally; [6]**physiology (of the brain):** functioning (of the brain) [7]**dominant:** more in control; [8]**stutter:** speak with repetition of initial word sounds: b-bb-boy; [9]**three-dimensional:** having height, width, and depth; [10]**random:** not in any organized sequence; [11]**resolve:** solve

Questions on the Model

1. What is the thesis statement? Double underline it.
2. Does this essay discuss mostly similarities, mostly differences, or both similarities and differences?
3. What is the topic of each body paragraph?

Comparison Structure Words and Phrases

When you want to compare something within a sentence or between two sentences, comparison structure words and phrases are useful. These words and phrases connect the two parts of a comparison of two items, places, persons, and so on. The following table gives a partial list of the most common words and phrases that are used to show similarities.

COMPARISON STRUCTURE WORDS AND PHRASES

| Sentence Connectors | Conjunctions | | Others | Paired Conjunctions |
	Coordinating	Subordinating		
similarly likewise also too	and . . . (too)	as just as	just like the same alike similar to the same as the same (as) equal equally	both . . . and not only . . . but also

Let's study each group of comparison structure words and phrases.

- Sentence connectors connect two independent clauses. All sentence connectors may be used with a period and a comma between the independent clauses.

  Tokyo is the financial heart of Japan. **Similarly**, New York is the center of banking and finance in the United States.

- Some sentence connectors may also be used with a semicolon and a comma between the independent clauses.

  Tokyo is the financial heart of Japan; **likewise**, New York is the center of banking and finance in the United States.

- The word *also* is generally not used with a semicolon. *Also* may appear in other positions in the second independent clause.

  Tokyo is a major financial center. New York is an important center of banking and finance **also**.
  Tokyo is the financial heart of Japan. New York is **also** an important center of banking and finance.

- The word *too* is usually placed at the end of the second independent clause. It is often used together with the coordinating conjunction *and*.

    Tokyo is a center of style and fashion. New York is, **too**.
    Tokyo is a center of style and fashion, **and** New York is, **too**.

- The subordinating conjunction *just as* begins a dependent clause.

    Tokyo is crowded and noisy **just as** New York is.
    Tokyo has traffic problems **just as** New York does.

- Notice the difference in usage between *just as* and *just like* in the "Others" list in the chart. Just as is a subordinating conjunction and is followed by a subject and a verb. *Just like* is a preposition and is followed by a noun or noun phrase.

    Tokyo is crowded and noisy **just as** New York is.
    Tokyo is crowded and noisy **just like** New York.

- Other comparison structure words and phrases are used to show comparisons within sentences. The part of speech for each comparison word or phrase is given in parenthesis.

    Tokyo's traffic is **similar to** New York's. (prepositions)
    The streets in downtown Tokyo and New York City are **alike.** (adjective)
    The subway system in New York City is **the same as** the one in Tokyo. (noun + preposition)
    The shopping areas are **the same.** (noun phrase)
    The exclusive shops in Tokyo display **the same** fashions **as** the exclusive shops in New York. (noun + preposition)
    Tokyo and New York City are **equally** crowded. (adverb)
    Tokyo and New York City have **equal** traffic problems.(adjective)

- Paired conjunctions are always used together. Notice that the word that comes after the second conjunction must be the same part of speech (noun, verb, prepositional phrase, etc.) as the word that comes after the first conjunction. This is an important rule in English and is called the rule of **parallelism**.

    Right: The two cities are both **noisy** (adjective) and **crowded** (adjective).
    Wrong: The two cities are both **busy** (adjective) and **have too many people** (verb phrase).

    Both **New York City** and **Tokyo** have outstanding international restaurants. (nouns)
    Tokyoites and New Yorkers can both **eat** and **drink** in any kind of restaurant. (verbs)
    The two cities have both **positive** and **negative** features. (adjectives)
    Not only **Tokyoites** but also **New Yorkers** dress fashionably. (nouns)
    You can see joggers not only **in Central Park** but also **in Hibuya Park.** (prepositional phrases)

ABOVE MATERIAL FROM: INTRODUCTION TO ACADEMIC WRITING

Practice

Comparison Words

Circle all of the words that show similarities in the model essay on page 62.

Practice

Paired Conjunctions

Complete the following sentences. Be sure to follow the rule of parallelism.

1. Both in Tokyo and ___*in New York City*___ the art museums display many famous masterpieces.

2. Both overcrowded subways and _____ are problems in Tokyo and New York City.

3. You can buy designer clothes not only in boutiques but also _____ .

4. New Yorkers and Tokyoites not only can see a movie but also _____ at any time.

5. In the summer, the weather in Tokyo and in New York is both hot and _____ .

6. The Ginza and Fifth Avenue shopping districts have both fine jewelers and _____ .

Practice

Using Comparison Structure Words and Phrases

Write a new sentence comparing the two sentences in each of the following pairs, using the given comparison structure words. Punctuate correctly.

1. Advertising brings the public information about a product or a service. It is used to sell an idea or an event. (similarly)

   ___*Advertising brings the public information about a product; similarly, it is used to*___

   ___*sell an idea or an event.*___

2. Advertisements influence a person's choice of food and other daily necessities. They influence a person's choice of vacation spots and restaurants. (not only . . . but also)

_____

_____

3. Advertising influences people's spending habits. It raises their standard of living. (both . . . and)

_____

_____

4. Advertising creates a desire for better clothing. Advertising creates a desire for a more attractive personal appearance. (not only . . . but also)

_____

_____

5. Newspaper and magazines are largely supported by advertising. Radio and television are largely supported by advertising. (just as)

_____

_____

6. Newspapers are important advertising media because they reach millions of readers. Magazines are important advertising media because they reach millions of readers. (like)

_____

_____

Practice

Sentence of Comparison

Write sentences of comparison using the given information.

1. The Spanish language/the Italian language/in grammar and vocabulary (similar to) ___ _The Spanish language_

   is similar to the Italian language in grammar and vocabulary.

2. Learning to speak English/learning to write English/important (both . . . and) _____

   _____

3. School sports are enjoyed/by male students/by female students (alike) _____

_____

4. A high school student who is continuing on to college/a high school student who is not going on to college/ graduation requirements. (the same . . . as) _____

_____

5. Private universities/public colleges/good education (and . . . too) _____

_____

6. Books at a private university/books at a public college/cost (the same as) _____

_____

7. Students in private colleges don't just study all the time/students in public colleges participate in sports, clubs, drama, music, and other extracurricular activities. (similarly) _____

_____

8. Exercising daily keeps a body strong/eating nutritious food/necessary for good health (likewise) _____

_____

Contrast Structure Words and Phrases

Now that you have learned to use comparison structure words and phrases to show how two things are the same, in this section you will learn to use contrast structure words and phrases to show how two things are different. These words and phrases connect the two parts of a contrast between two items, places, persons, and so on. The following table gives a partial list of the most common words and phrases that are used to show differences.

CONTRAST STRUCTURE WORDS AND PHRASES

| Sentence Connectors | Conjunctions | | Others |
	Coordinating	Subordinating	
on the other hand	but	although even though	different from unlike
in contrast	yet	while	
however		whereas	

Now let's study each group of contrast structure words and phrases.

- Remember that sentence connectors connect two independent clauses. Contrast sentence connectors may be used with either a period and a comma or a semicolon and a comma between the independent clauses:

  Men excel at math. In contrast, women are better at language.
  Men excel at math; on the other hand, women are better at language.

- The two coordinating conjunctions in the chart have slightly different uses.

1. Use *but* when the information in the second clause is in complete contrast to the information in the first clause.

   Men listen primarily with their right ear, but women listen with both ears.

2. Use *yet* when the information in the second clause is unexpected or surprising.

   The language center is in the left side of the brain in both sexes; **yet** women have stronger language skills than men.

   NOTE: You can use *but* in place of *yet*.

   The language center is in the left side of the brain in both sexes, **but** women have stronger language skills than men.

- Subordinating conjunctions begin a dependent clause. There are differences in meaning and comma use between the two pairs of contrast subordinators in the chart.

1. Use *although/even though* when the result in the independent clause is an unexpected surprise because of the information given in the dependent clause.

   Even though I took the driving test three times, I couldn't pass it. I couldn't pass the driving test **although** I took it three times.

2. Use *while/whereas* when the information in the first clause is in strong contrast (direct opposition) to the information in the second clause.

   Some people like to exercise indoors, **while** others prefer to exercise outdoors.
   Whereas some people like to exercise indoors, others prefer to exercise outdoors.

   Notice that a comma is placed after the independent clause before *while* or *whereas* to show contrast (direct opposition). This is an exception to the usual rule.

- The two other contrast structure words in the "Others" list are prepositions and are used as follows:

   Men's spatial abilities are **different from** women's (spatial abilities).
   Men are **different from** women in their spatial skills.
   Women's spatial abilities are **unlike** men's (spatial abilities).
   Unlike men, women use both ears to listen.

Practice

Contrast Structure Words

A. *Circle all of the words that show contrast in the model essay on page 62.*

B. *Write contrast sentences using the given information. Use a coordinator, a subordinator, and a sentence connector.*

1. Jose swims well. Maria swims poorly.

   a. *Jose swims well, but Maria swims poorly.*

   b. *Jose swims well, whereas Maria swims poorly.*

   c. *Jose swims well; however, Maria swims poorly.*

2. Fresh fruit and vegetables taste delicious. Canned fruits and vegetables are tasteless.

   a. _____

   b. _____

   c. _____

3. Eating well and exercising will keep you in good health. Exercising by itself will not.

   a. _____

   b. _____

   c. _____

4. A university has a graduate school. A college usually does not.

   a. _____

   b. _____

   c. _____

5. Mark will go to college on a full scholarship. Carlos will have to work part time.

   a. _____

   b. _____

   c. _____

6. In England, medical care is free. In the United States, people must pay for medical care.

   a. _____

   b. _____

   c. _____

Practice

Contrast Sentences

A. *Complete the following sentences. Punctuate correctly.*

1. I love to go camping, but _my sister doesn't._ _____ .

2. Betty has gained ten pounds yet _____

   _____

3. She should exercise although _____

   _____

4. _____

   _____ whereas Susan jogs every day.

5. Climbing mountains is great exercise. On the other hand _____

   _____

6. Living on an island is different from _____

   _____

B. *Work with a partner. Take turns saying and writing sentences showing differences between men and women. Use the contrast structure words in parentheses.*

1. (on the other hand) _____

   _____

2. (while) _____

   _____

ABOVE MATERIAL FROM: INTRODUCTION TO ACADEMIC WRITING

COMPARISON–CONTRAST

This is the pattern a writer uses to show how two things are similar and/or different.
A *comparison* can include:

- only similarities
- similarities *and* differences.

ABOVE MATERIAL FROM: MORE READING POWER

A *contrast* includes only the differences.

Some signal words for the comparison-contrast pattern:

Signals of difference:

however	but	unlike	on the other hand
in contrast	while	although	conversely
instead	yet	rather	different from
more than	less than		

Comparative forms of adjectives and adverbs are also used to signal difference (older, faster).

Signals of similarity:

like	both	similarly	in the same way
as	same	also	in common

EXAMPLE A: Comparison (Similarities and Differences)

Both New York City and Paris depend on vast subway lines to transport their millions of commuters. In both cities, the subways are often crowded, especially at rush hours. Another likeness is the terrible noise level in the trains. A further similarity is that the two subway systems both cover a wide area at little expense for commuters. However, the differences between the two are quite striking. While subway stations in New York range from plain to ugly, Paris stations are generally attractive. Many of the French stations are filled with works of art. In Paris, the subway trains are clean and they run every few minutes. On the other hand, New York's trains can sometimes be less clean and reliable.

Does this paragraph include similarities, differences, or (both)?

Main Idea: _____

_____

Signal Words	*Examples*
Both	_____
both	_____
Another likeness	_____
A further similarity	_____
However	_____
While	_____
On the other hand	_____

EXAMPLE B: Comparison (Similarities)

   Can you think of anything that Ukraine and Japan have in common? Not much, except for one surprising aspect of their cooking. Ukrainians are fond of a dish called *pilmeni*. It is made of pieces of flat pastry folded around a spicy meat filling. The Japanese make a dish that is remarkably like it, only they call it *gyoza*. In both countries, furthermore, people like to eat their *pilmeni* or their *gyoza* with sauce. The Ukrainians use sour cream and the Japanese use soy sauce.

Main Idea: _____

_____

Does this paragraph include (similarities,) differences, or both?

Signal Words	*Examples*
in common	_____
like it	_____
both	_____

EXAMPLE C: Contrast (Differences)

   When the first baby arrives in a household, everything changes. <u>While before</u>, the mother needed an alarm clock in the morning, <u>now</u> the baby decides when she should wake up. <u>Formerly</u>, the parents spent their evenings watching TV or reading, <u>but not now</u>. All their free time is spent admiring their infant. <u>In contrast</u> to pre-baby days, their life is more carefully planned. <u>While they used to</u> go out to see friends whenever they wanted to, that is not possible <u>any more</u>. If they want to go out without the baby, they must arrange for a babysitter. <u>Unlike</u> the neat and tidy rooms of the past, these days their apartment is full of baby things. Their friends have even noticed a <u>difference</u> in the topic of conversation: it's always about the baby!

Main Idea: _____

_____

Does this paragraph include similarities, (differences,) or both?

Signal Words	*Examples*
While before	_____
now	_____
Formerly	_____
not now	_____

In contrast	_____
While they used to	_____
any more	_____
Unlike	_____
difference	_____

Exercise 1

In these paragraphs, the signal words are not underlined. Read each paragraph. Underline the signal words. Then write the main idea and the signal words and examples on the lines below. Compare your work with another student.

MODERN VERSIONS OF FAMILIAR MACHINES

1. The latest kind of vending machine is nothing like the vending machines of the past. Like the old machines, the new ones are a quick and convenient way to buy food. But the new machines have been improved in several important ways. The old machines worked with coins that were sometimes "swallowed" without providing your food. The new machines, however, work with plastic cards that can be used many times without error. The food supplied by the old machines was usually not very good: stale pastries or tasteless sandwiches. In contrast, the new machines sell all kinds of delicious meals. They may offer fresh, oven-baked pizza, espresso coffee, or fresh pasta. In general, these new machines sell more interesting and better-tasting food.

Main Idea: _____

_____

Does this paragraph include similarities, differences, or both?

Signal Words	*Examples*
_____	_____
_____	_____
_____	_____
_____	_____

2. The so-called "portable" computers of just a few years ago were heavy machines. They weighed about 15 pounds and were really designed to stay in one place. The idea of traveling with an old "portable" was out of the question. It would not even fit under an airline seat. Present-day laptop computers, however, are totally different. These "portables" are really meant to be carried around. They are sometimes even called "notebooks." Unlike the heavy monsters of the past, the laptop computers weigh only about five pounds. They can fit easily

into a briefcase. In spite of their size, though, they have much more memory capacity than the older computers. Surprisingly, the laptops also have larger screens than the older models.

Main Idea: _____

_____

Does this paragraph include similarities, differences, or both?

Signal Words   *Examples*

_____   _____

_____   _____

_____   _____

3. The next big technological change will be the shift from gasoline to electric-powered automobiles. In some ways, the cars are quite similar. Like gasoline cars, the electric vehicles provide convenient, private transportation. The interior of the two vehicles is much the same. Steering, brakes, and wheels are not different. On the other hand, there is a major difference. Unlike gasoline cars, the electric vehicle is totally silent. In contrast to the sound of the ignition in a gasoline engine, the sound of starting an electric car is "click." There is no engine sound, either, in the electric car.

Main Idea: _____

_____

Does this paragraph include similarities, differences, or both?

Signal Words   *Examples*

_____   _____

_____   _____

_____   _____

_____   _____

Exercise 2

Read each paragraph. Underline the signal words. Then write the main idea and the signal words and details on the lines below. Compare your work with another student.

IDEAS ABOUT EDUCATION

1. High school graduates are sometimes nervous about attending college, because they fear that everything will be different. In fact, there are some important similarities between college and high school. In both places, academic success depends on being a responsible student. This means attending classes regularly, doing your homework, and studying new materials carefully. Similarly, social success in college is like high school. If you have had friends in high school, chances are you will have friends in college, too. College also resembles high school in student activities. Musical groups, sports teams, special interest clubs, and other activities are found in both institutions.

Main Idea: _____

_____

Does this paragraph include similarities, differences, or both?

Signal Words   *Examples*

_____   _____

_____   _____

_____   _____

_____   _____

2. The University of Bologna in northern Italy is different from most North American universities. One important difference is its age. Founded in the tenth century, it is the oldest university in Europe. Its ancient halls give students a strong sense of history. This is in sharp contrast to the usual attitude of American students who study in newer surroundings. The University of Bologna is different, as well, because of its location. While North American universities are often located outside the city center, Bologna's campus is in the heart of the city. Unlike the American university campus, there are no trees or open spaces near this old Italian institution. Instead, students meet on the streets, in cafes, and in the courtyards of the historic buildings.

Main Idea: _____

_____

Does this paragraph include similarities, differences, or both?

Signal Words   *Examples*

_____   _____

_____   _____

_____   _____

_____   _____

Writing Personal and Business Letters

Personal Letters

Letters to friends and relatives are informal letters. These letters do not have to be typed, and they usually follow the form below.

> May 8, 1998 — date
>
> Dear Daniel, — greeting
>
> Thank you very much for the wonderful holiday vacation I spent with you and your family. Your mother is such a terrific cook! I think I must have gained 10 pounds in just the week I spent with you. I really appreciate your taking time off from work to take me around and show me so many places. You are lucky to live in such an interesting area. I hope that soon you will be able to visit my part of the country. Thank you again for a wonderful time. Let's keep in touch. — message
>
> closing — Best regards,
> signature — Matthew

Remember these guidelines when you write a personal letter:

1. The date goes in the upper right corner. (The month is capitalized, and a comma goes between the day and the year.)
2. The greeting (Dear _____) is followed by a comma.
3. The closing (often "Love" in personal letters) is followed by a comma.

Don't forget:

1. The return address of the person who writes the letter goes in the upper left corner.
2. The address (the address of the person who will receive the letter) goes in the center of the envelope.
3. The stamp goes in the upper right corner.

Ready to Write

Practice Writing Personal Letters

Write a letter to one of the following on a separate piece of paper. Bring your finished letter to class in a properly addressed envelope.

- A friend. Invite him or her to come visit you.
- Your aunt. Thank her for the gift she sent you.
- A friend you haven't seen recently. Tell him or her what is new in your life.
- Your parents. Tell them about an important decision you have made.

Business Letters

Business letters are formal letters. The form of a business letter is different from the form of a personal letter. Look at the sample business letter below. Notice the differences between it and the personal letter on page 77.

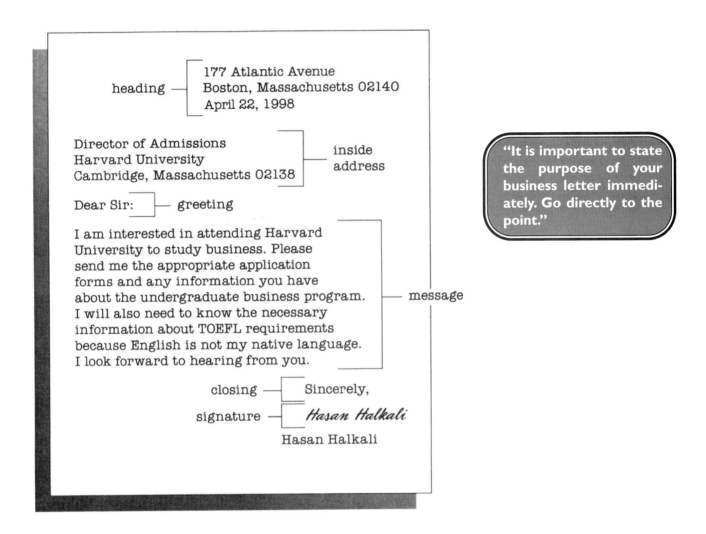

heading —
177 Atlantic Avenue
Boston, Massachusetts 02140
April 22, 1998

Director of Admissions
Harvard University
Cambridge, Massachusetts 02138 — inside address

Dear Sir: — greeting

I am interested in attending Harvard University to study business. Please send me the appropriate application forms and any information you have about the undergraduate business program. I will also need to know the necessary information about TOEFL requirements because English is not my native language. I look forward to hearing from you. — message

closing — Sincerely,
signature — Hasan Halkali
Hasan Halkali

"It is important to state the purpose of your business letter immediately. Go directly to the point."

Remember these guidelines for writing business letters:

1. The greeting is followed by a colon.
2. It is important to state the purpose of your letter immediately. Go directly to the point. Be as brief and explicit as you can.
3. Type business letters if possible.
4. Do not ask personal information (age, health, family) of the person you are writing to.
5. Do not use contractions.

Ready to Write

Practice Writing Business Letters

ACTIVITY 1

Read the advertisement for the Philadelphia Orchestra. Write a letter requesting tickets. Use the information below to help you. In your letter you will need to state

1. whether you want a matinee or an evening performance.
2. the date of the performance you want to attend.
3. which price ticket you want.
4. whether you are including your credit card number or a personal check.

Make your letter short and to the point.

ACTIVITY 2

Do one of the following. Bring your finished letter to class in a properly addressed envelope. (Use the same format for a business letter envelope that you use for a personal letter envelope.)

- Write your own letter to a college admissions office asking for information.
- Write to a radio station requesting more information about a product you heard advertised.
- Write a letter stating that you ordered a magazine subscription three months ago and haven't received any copies of the magazine yet.
- Write a letter to a university informing the director of admissions that you have decided not to attend that university.

Answering these questions will help you.

1. Have you included both a heading and an inside address? Are they in the proper places?
2. Is there a colon after the greeting?
3. Is your letter direct and to the point?
4. Is the closing followed by a comma?
5. Did you sign your letter?

Ready to Write

Use Your Imagination

Imagine yourself in the following situation:

> Two weeks ago you called the person who lives above you in your apartment building. You were upset because he plays his stereo so loudly. He plays it very loudly all day long so it bothers you when you are trying to study. He also plays it late at night when you are trying to sleep. When you

SEE THE Philadelphia Orchestra

Academy of Music
1420 Locust St., Phila., Pa. 19102

Hurry! Order tickets now!

EVENINGS–8 PM
MATINEES–Wed, Sat and Sun 3 PM

PRICES

	ORCHESTRA & MEZZANINE	BALCONY
EVENINGS		
MON-THURS	$30	$25
FRI-SAT	$32	$27
MATINEES		
SAT	$27	$22
SUN	$30	$25
WED	$25	$20

spoke with him on the phone, he said that he would try to keep the volume lower. The first few days it was better, but now it is becoming a problem again. Also, you are trying to study for your final exam. It is very difficult because of the constant noise.

1. Write a polite letter to him asking him to please be more considerate.

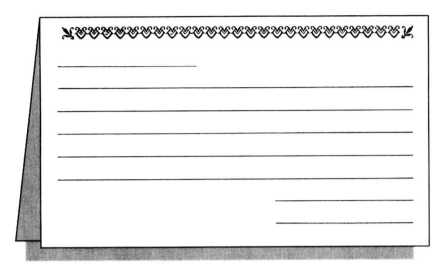

2. It is now one week later and the noise has gotten even worse. You are furious. Write an angry letter to your landlord threatening to break your lease and move out if he does not do something about the noise. Since this is a business letter, don't forget the heading and the inside address. Remember to type the final copy of a business letter.

Separating Formal from Informal Phrases

In each pair of sentences or phrases below, one should be used only in informal letters. The other phrase is appropriate for formal letters. Put an F in front of the one that is formal and an I in front of the one that is informal.

1. _____ I'm really sorry about what happened.

   _____ I would like to apologize for any inconvenience this may have caused you.

2. _____ I look forward to hearing from you soon.

   _____ I can't wait to hear from you.

3. _____ Dear Julie,

   _____ Dear Mrs. Brody:

4. _____ Yours truly,

   _____ Love,

5. _____ I will call you Monday morning.

   _____ I'll give you a call next week.

6. _____ I appreciate your help in this matter.

   _____ Thanks a lot for helping me.

You Be the Editor

Read the following memo from the president of Bayview Associates. The form is correct for a memo but there are eight mistakes. Correct the mistakes and rewrite the memo correctly.

MEMO

TO: All Employees
FROM: David Stanson, President
DATE: 3/13/98
RE: Punctuality

it has come recently to my attention that we are becoming increasingly lax about beginning our work day in 9 a.m. I understand that many of you are always on time and I thank you for your reliability, I also realize that sometimes lateness cannot be avoided. I feel, however, that habitual late has become a serious problem and that I must mention it before it gets worser. It is my opinion that we are a team and that we must all work together to build strongest company we can. Inattention to punctuality creates resentment among coworkers. I will appreciate it if you paying more attention to this important detail in the future.

ABOVE MATERIAL FROM: READY TO WRITE MORE

THEMATIC READING SECTION

Human Behavior

Brain Power

Do You Know Your Right Brain from Your Left?

1   The human brain is divided into two sides, or hemispheres, called the right brain and the left brain. The two hemispheres work together, but each one specializes in certain ways of thinking. Each side has its own way of using information to help us think, understand, and process information.

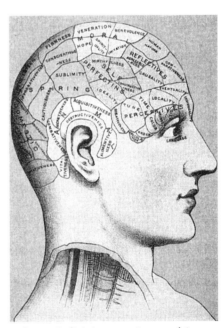

2   The left side of the brain controls language. It is more verbal and logical. It names things and puts them into groups. It uses rules and likes ideas to be clear, logical, and orderly. It is best at speech, reading, writing, and math. You use this side of the brain when you memorize spelling and grammar rules or when you do a math problem.

3   The right side of the brain is more visual and creative. It specializes in using information it receives from the senses of sight, sound, smell, touch, and taste. This side of the brain likes to dream and experiment. It controls your appreciation of music, color, and art. You use this side when you draw a picture or listen to music.

4   Although we all use both sides of our brains, one side is usually stronger or dominant. Some people are more "left-brained," and others are more "right-brained." Our dominant side influences the kinds of jobs and hobbies we have. Politicians, artists, architects, and musicians depend on their right brains. Accountants, engineers, doctors, and lawyers usually rely on their left brains.

Are You Right-Brained or Left-Brained? Reprinted courtesy of *Teen* Magazine, November 1993 issue.

SELECTION 1

Building Reading Skills

Identifying Main Ideas

Which of the following topics are discussed in the article? Put a check mark next to those topics.

_____✓___ 1. the side of the brain that is more logical

_____ 2. the size and weight of the human brain

___✓___ 3. the side of the brain that is more creative

___✓___ 4. the types of people that are usually right-brained or left-brained

_____ 5. the part of the brain that controls muscular activity

_____ 6. diseases of the brain

Building Reading Skills

Locating Main Ideas

Answer the following questions by writing the number of the paragraph on the lines provided.

1. Which paragraph describes the left brain? (¶_____2_____)

2. Which paragraph explains that the human brain is divided into two sides? (¶_____1_____)

3. Which paragraph discusses the kind of people who are usually left-brained or right-brained? (¶_____4_____)

4. Which paragraph describes the right brain? (¶_____3_____)

How Well Did You Read?

Read the following statements. If a statement is true, write T *on the line provided. If it is false, write* F.

__T__ 1. The human brain has two sides.

__F__ 2. Everyone is more right-brained than left-brained.

__T__ 3. The right side of the brain is more creative.

__T__ 4. When you solve a math problem, you use your left brain.

__F__ 5. Both sides of the brain specialize in the same things.

__T__ 6. Artists use their right brain more than engineers do.

__F__ 7. When you paint a picture, you use your left brain.

Application of Information

Read the following descriptions of four different people. Decide who you think is left-brained and who is right-brained. Write Left *next to the descriptions of left-brained people and* Right *next to the descriptions of right-brained people.*

Right **1.** Daniel's hobby is drawing cartoons. He loves surprises and hates following a strict schedule. He is very sensitive and likes to find new ways of doing things.

Left **2.** Dr. Curley is very careful about keeping his appointments. He is always on time and does things in an orderly way. Every day, as soon as he gets home from work, he takes his dog for a walk and goes jogging for a half hour.

Left **3.** Debbie is a lawyer at a big law firm in New York. Her language skills are very good. She is a very logical person. She gets up, eats, and goes to sleep at the same time every day.

Right **4.** Ian Baker is the mayor of a small city. He is always looking for creative ways to solve the city's problems. In his spare time, he enjoys going to concerts and playing the piano.

Expanding Vocabulary

Complete each sentence with a word from the list.

hemispheres	specializes	information	verbal
rules	memorize	logical	creative
dominant			

1. Artists are _____creative_____ people.

2. Our brains have two _____hemispheres_____.

3. The left side of an accountant's brain is probably _____dominant_____.

4. English spelling _____rules_____ are very complicated.

5. _____verbal_____ people have good language skills. → *destreza*

6. Each side of the brain uses _____information_____ in a different way.

7. The right side of the brain _____specializes_____ in using knowledge it gets from the senses.
   conocimiento. *sentido.*

8. The lawyer gave a _____logical_____ argument. It made sense.

9. It is difficult to _____memorize_____ all the English grammar rules.

> **FYI** Cats can catch rabbits even though rabbits are faster. This is because cats are smarter than rabbits. They have a better brain.

SELECTION 2

Albert Einstein is one of the most famous scientists of the twentieth century. He was born in 1879 in Germany and became a U.S. citizen in 1940. Einstein received the Nobel Prize in physics in 1921. His theories have changed the way we think about the universe and the dimensions of time and space. Read the following article, **Albert Einstein: The Man and the Legends about Him**, to learn more about the life of this great man.

Before You Read

Prereading Discussion

1. Write the first five words that come into your mind when you think of the word *genius*.

_____

_____

_____

_____

Compare your list with your classmates' lists.

2. Have you ever known someone whom you think is a genius? In what area? How would you describe this person? What qualities did he or she have that were special?

_____

_____

_____

_____

_____

_____

_____

_____

Albert Einstein: The Man and the Legends about Him

1   Albert Einstein's early childhood would not lead anyone to predict that he would become the most famous and influential physicist of his time. He did not talk at all until the age of three, late in almost any culture. One "legend" has it that young Albert finally broke his silence at the supper table one night saying, "The soup is too hot." His parents asked why he had never said a word until then, and Albert replied, "Because up to now everything was alright."

2   Einstein was born in Ulm, Württemberg, Germany in 1879. He disliked his early years in school and studied primarily at home. His limitless curiosity showed up in questions like, "Why does a compass needle always point in the same direction?" at the age of five, and, "What would the world look like if I rode on a beam of light?" at age 14. He never lost his curiosity. As an adult he said, "The most beautiful thing we can experience is the mysterious. It is the source of all true art and science."

3   In 1905, Einstein published four papers which revolutionized modern physics. In 1915, he published his general theory of relativity. His famous equation $E = mc^2$ (energy equals mass times the velocity of light squared) is a cornerstone of the modern nuclear age. And he won the Nobel prize for physics in 1921.

4   Einstein was of Jewish descent, and in 1933 the Nazi government of Germany took away his property and citizenship. He then moved to the United States.

5   Einstein became a member of the staff of the Institute for Advanced Studies in Princeton, New Jersey. In 1944, he became an American citizen. He lived a quiet personal life. He enjoyed classical music, and played the violin. After a session with a group of fellow musicians, one of them was reported to have said, "He'd be a good musician if only he could count!" An interesting comment to make about a man whose life work involved highly complex mathematical thinking.

6   Einstein kept his sense of humor throughout his life. A magazine called *Scientific American* once had a competition for the best explanation of the theory of relativity in three thousand words. Einstein said, "I'm the only one in my entire circle of friends who is not entering. I don't believe I could do it."

How Well Did You Read?

Read the following statements. If a statement is true, write T *on the line. If it is false, write* F.

_____ **1.** Einstein learned to talk at a very early age.

_____ **2.** As a child, Einstein was very curious, and he continued to be curious throughout his life.

Albert Einstein: The Man and the Legends about Him. The following adaptation is reprinted with the permission of *Provoking Thoughts* (Austin, Minnesota), from the May–June 1991 issue.

_____ **3.** Einstein's theory of relativity revolutionized physics.

_____ **4.** Einstein was born in Germany. He lived there his entire life.

_____ **5.** Einstein had a good sense of humor.

_____ **6.** He had a very active social life.

_____ **7.** One of Einstein's hobbies was playing the violin.

_____ **8.** Albert Einstein won the Nobel prize for physics.

Building Reading Skills

Scanning For Details

Read the following questions about Albert Einstein. Then scan the article to find the answers. Work as quickly as possible.
Do not reread every word in the article. As soon as you find the answer to a question, move on to the next one.

1. Where was Einstein born? _____

2. When did he publish his papers about the theory of relativity? _____ .

3. What prize did he win in 1921? _____ .

4. What musical instrument did Einstein play? _____ .

5. When did he become an American citizen? _____ .

Building Vocabulary Skills

Word Forms

Complete each sentence with the correct word.

1. predict   predictions

   a. Can you _____ what this article will be about?

   b. Some people like to make _____ about the future.

2. mysterious   mystery

   a. No one could figure out how the fire started. It is a _____ .

   b. I don't know Dr. Brown very well. But he seems like a _____ person.

3. curious   curiosity

    a. Einstein was _____ about the world around him.

    b. Have you ever heard the expression "_____ killed the cat, satisfaction brought it back"?

4. beauty   beautiful

    a. My French teacher is one of the most _____ women I have ever seen.

    b. Do you agree with the expression, "_____ is only skin deep"?

5. mathematical   math

    a. Einstein's work involved highly complex _____ concepts.

    b. Joe's favorite subject in school is _____ .

6. competition   competes

    a. My brother _____ in the Boston Marathon every year.

    b. Eric entered a poem in the school poetry _____.

SELECTION 3

How Good Is Your Memory? is an interview with a teacher and psychotherapist, Diane Englund. Through her work, Ms. Englund has learned that different people gather and remember information in different ways. This observation has led her to an interest in how the brain processes and remembers information.

Before You Read

Prereading Activity

Before you read the following interview about memory, think about the types of things that are easy or difficult for you to remember. Put E next to the items below that are easy for you to remember. Put D next to the ones that are difficult for you to remember.

_____ names	_____ phone numbers	_____ statistics
_____ words to songs	_____ addresses	_____ directions
_____ math formulas	_____ speeches	_____ birthdays
_____ faces	_____ sports	_____ historical facts

How Good Is Your Memory?

What aspects of brain biology interest you?

1   I have become very interested in the importance of memory in our lives. Most people know that the brain controls how the body works. The brain also controls what the mind thinks, how we feel, how we process information, and how we perceive things. I am interested in how people remember, what they remember, and how they use and improve their memories.

What can you tell us about memory?

2   Memory plays an important role in learning and thinking. People have different abilities to remember. Stress, fatigue, emotional problems, and illness can decrease the ability to remember. General good health contributes to good memory. Practice also improves memory. For example, the more math facts you learn, the easier math facts are to learn. The same is true with music. The more songs you listen to and learn, the easier it becomes. People gather and remember information in different ways. Some people remember colors or smells or sounds. Other people find it easier to remember spoken words. While still others remember printed words easily.

Are there different kinds of memory?

3   Yes. The two basic categories are long-term memory and short-term memory. Long-term memory is the ability to remember events from the distant past. Long-term memory is often the strongest and lasts throughout a person's life. One kind of long-term memory is called "screen memory." This means that many experiences get put together in the mind as one memory. For example, in your memory you might have only one "picture" of a childhood trip to the doctor's office. This one memory, however, is probably a combination of many trips to the doctor.

4   Short-term memory is the ability to remember events in the recent past, for example the name of someone you met at a party last night. Short-term memory is often challenged by stress, illness, and aging. Many of us have, or have had, grandparents who remember events from their childhood with great accuracy, but are unable to remember what happened yesterday. Most people can only remember seven items in sequence. This is why telephone numbers, for example, are typically seven digits long.

Are all memories accurate?

5   No, not all memories are correct, but they all tell us something about the person who is doing the remembering. The memory may tell us what the rememberer likes or dislikes, what he or she wishes, and it may also tell us about his or her fears. The study of memory may also provide information about the health or illness of a person. This is a very exciting frontier in biological science. There is still a lot for us to learn.

Why is it easier for people to remember some things and more difficult for them to remember other things?

6   That's a good question. It's easier to remember things that have emotional meaning to you. It's also easier to remember information that you practice and use a lot. Repetition reinforces memory; the more you repeat something, the better you remember it. Some people have very visual memories. That is, they remember things they see. In fact, it is often easier to remember information that comes to us through more than one of our five senses.

How Well Did You Read?

Read the following statements. If a statement is true, write T *on the line. If it is false, write* F.

_____   **1.**   The state of your health can affect your ability to remember things accurately.

How Good Is Your Memory? Interview printed with the permission of Diane Englund.

ABOVE MATERIAL FROM: FOR YOUR INFORMATION I

_____ 2. All people gather and remember information in the same way

_____ 3. The two basic kinds of memory are long-term memory and screen memory.

_____ 4. Short-term memory is the ability to remember things in the recent past.

_____ 5. Scientists have already discovered almost everything there is to know about memory.

_____ 6. The brain controls not only the way the body works but also the way the mind thinks.

_____ 7. We can learn many things by examining what a person remembers.

Expanding Vocabulary

Cross out the word in each group that does not belong.

1. stress	fatigue	illness	practice
2. think	jump	feel	perceive
3. kinds	categories	trips	groups
4. sequence	order	memory	series
5. typically	usually	generally	rarely
6. correct	wrong	accurate	true

Using Examples

Authors often use examples to support their ideas. In her interview, Ms. Englund used several examples to support her ideas and make them easier to understand. Look back through the interview and find the examples she used to support the following points.

1. Screen memory is a combination of many experiences that get put together in the mind as one memory.

_____

_____

2. Most people can only remember seven items in sequence.

_____

_____

3. Practice improves memory.

_____

The brain of an average adult male weighs 3 pounds 2.2 ounces (1.42 kilograms). The average woman's brain weighs 2 pounds 6 ounces (1.08 kilograms). There is no correlation between brain weight and intelligence.

TYING IT ALL TOGETHER

Discussion

1. Swiss philosopher Henri-Frédéric Amiel once said, "To do easily what is difficult for others is the mark of talent. To do what is impossible for talented people is the mark of genius." What do you think he meant? Do you agree with him?

2. Most people think it's wonderful to have a good memory, but there may be some things you wish you could forget. Alexander Durivage, author and historian, stated this idea very well when he said, "They teach us to remember; why don't they teach us to forget? Memory can be a curse as well as a blessing." Discuss this quote with your classmates. Do you have some memories you wish you could forget?

3. Thomas Edison is famous for inventing the electric light bulb and the phonograph. He believed, "Genius is one percent inspiration and 99 percent perspiration." What do you think?

Self-Test

Complete the sentences with words from the list.

specializes	compete
logical	predicts - Pronosticar.
sequence - Serie.	entire - Entero. Completo.
accurate - exacto - Preciso	creative
mystery	memorize
curious	combination
verbal - Oral.	perceive - Percatarse - Concientizarse.
contribute	

1. The cause of the fire is still a _____ . No one knows how it started.

2. The radio station plays a _____ of classical music, rock and roll, and jazz.

3. Harvey is a doctor. He _____ in problems of the heart.

4. Juliette is a very _____ child. Although she is only two years old, she already speaks in complete sentences.

5. Not many people can read an _____ book in one day.

6. Some people find it difficult to _____ speeches. They prefer to refer to their notes.

7. The police are trying to discover the _____ of events that happened on the night of the murder.

8. Every four years, soccer teams from around the world _____ for the World Cup.

9. When I looked at the twins, I couldn't _____ any difference between them. They looked exactly the same to me. However, their parents can tell them apart easily.

10. Judy received a package in the mail. She was so _____ about what was inside that she opened it up immediately.

11. Eating well and getting exercise _____ to good health.

12. The weatherman says it won't be a good day for a picnic. He _____ that it will rain.

13. This clock never tells the correct time. It's not very _____ .

14. Jim is a musician. He also likes to paint and write poetry. All his friends think he is a very

_____ person.

15. Matt is left-brained. He is a mathematician and his thinking is always very _____ .

Reader's Journal

Think about the topics that you have read about and discussed in this unit. Choose a topic and write about it for ten to twenty minutes. You may pick a topic from the following list, or you may choose one of your own. Or you could write your reaction to one of the quotations you read in this unit.

UNIT 7

Are You Superstitious?

SELECTION 1

Before You Read

Prereading Activity

A. *Look at the following photographs. Match the picture with the correct caption.*

2. _____

1. _____   3. _____   4. _____

a. Walking under a ladder brings bad luck.
b. Don't open an umbrella indoors.
c. Make a wish and cross your fingers.
d. Protect yourself! Knock on wood.

B. *The following article is taken from the* World Book Encyclopedia. *On the lines provided, make a list of the topics you think will be discussed in the article. After you have finished reading the whole article, check to see how accurate your predictions were.*

_____

_____

_____

_____

_____

First Reading

Skimming

Skim each part of the article quickly without using a dictionary. Do not worry about specific details since you are only reading for the main ideas. Underline anything that seems important as you read. When you finish each part, answer the questions that follow.

Superstitions

1   **Superstition** is a traditional belief that a certain action or event can cause or foretell an apparently unrelated event. For example, some superstitious people believe that carrying a rabbit's foot will bring them good luck. Others believe that if a black cat crosses their path, they will have bad luck. To yet other superstitious people, dropping a knife or fork on the floor means company is coming. Such beliefs are superstitions because in each case the action and the event it foretells are traditionally thought to be connected. For instance, the rabbit's foot is associated with fertility.

2   Superstitions have existed in every human society throughout history. Most people, including highly educated individuals, act superstitiously from time to time. Many persons may joke about avoiding bad luck by knocking on wood or not walking under a ladder. But they have such beliefs anyway. Scholars once believed that all superstitions dated back to humanity's early history. But many superstitions have appeared in relatively recent times. According to a superstition in baseball, for example, a pitcher will give up a hit if anyone mentions that a no-hit game is being pitched.

3   Countless human activities are involved in superstitions. They include eating, sleeping, working, playing, getting married, having a baby, becoming ill, and dying. Times of danger and uncertainty have brought many superstitions. Superstitions concern animals, clothing, lakes, mountains, names, numbers, the planets and stars, the weather, and parts of the body.

Superstitions. From *The World Book Encyclopedia* © 1994 World Book, Inc. By permission of the publisher.

ABOVE MATERIAL FROM: FOR YOUR INFORMATION 2

How Well Did You Read?

Put a check mark (✓) next to the statements that are true.

_____ **1.** A superstition is a belief that a certain action can cause another unrelated action.

_____ **2.** Only a few societies throughout history have had superstitions.

_____ **3.** Although scholars used to think all superstitions were very old, many of them are relatively new.

_____ **4.** There are superstitions about almost every aspect of life.

4   **Kinds of superstitions.** Many superstitions deal with important events in a person's life, such as birth, entering adulthood, marriage, pregnancy, and death. Such superstitions supposedly ensure that a person will pass safely from one stage of life to the next. For example, a person born on Sunday will always have good luck. A bride and groom will have bad luck if they see each other on their wedding day before the ceremony. A pregnant woman must eat the right food, or she will give her child an unwanted birthmark. After a person dies, the doors and windows of the room should be opened so the spirit can leave.

5   Some superstitions involve a type of magic. One form of such magic comes from the belief that similar actions produce similar results. Many people believe a newborn baby must be carried upstairs before being carried downstairs. In this way, the child will be assured of rising in the world and having success. The same principle appears in the custom of putting money in a purse or wallet being given as a gift. The giver wants to make sure the purse or wallet will always contain money.

6   A number of superstitions involve someone's taking a deliberate action to cause something to happen or to prevent something from occurring. Most of these *causal* superstitions involve ensuring good luck, avoiding bad luck, or making something good happen. For example, carrying a silver dollar supposedly brings good luck. Some people will not start a trip on a Friday, especially if it is the 13th day of the month. Friday and the number 13 are both associated with bad luck. According to a Japanese belief, the number 4 is unlucky. This is because *shi*, the Japanese word for that number, sounds like the Japanese word that means *death*. As a result, many buildings in Japan have no fourth floor. According to another superstition, wedding guests throw rice at the newlyweds to ensure that the marriage will result in many children. Causal superstitions may involve actions intended to give bad luck to someone. Witches supposedly perform some of these actions.

7   Other superstitions foretell an event without any conscious action by the person involved. Some of these sign superstitions foretell good or bad luck. For example, finding a horseshoe or a four-leaf clover means good luck. Breaking a mirror or spilling salt brings bad luck. Other sign superstitions foretell a certain event or condition. A ring around the moon means rain will soon fall. A howling dog means death is near. A person with red hair has a quick temper.

8   Some sign superstitions may be changed into causal superstitions. If a person hangs a horseshoe over a door, witches cannot enter. If a young woman pins a four-leaf clover to her door, she will marry the first bachelor who comes in the door. In some cases, a person may avoid the bad luck involved in a sign superstition by taking immediate action. For example, someone who has spilled salt may cancel the bad luck by throwing a pinch of salt over the left shoulder.

How Well Did You Read?

Circle the letter of the word or phrase that best completes each statement.

1. Superstitions may involve _____ .
   a. magic
   b. important events in a person's life
   c. taking an action to cause or prevent something else
   d. (*all of the above*)

2. All of the following are causal superstitions except _____ .
   a. carrying a silver dollar to bring good luck
   b. finding a four-leaf clover means good luck
   c. throwing rice at newlyweds so they will have lots of children
   d. not starting a trip on Friday to avoid bad luck

3. Sign superstitions _____ .
   a. cannot be changed into causal superstitions
   b. are very rare
   c. do not involve deliberate action by the person involved
   d. deal with important events in a person's life

9   **The role of superstitions.** Many people scoff at superstitions because they consider such beliefs to be unscientific. However, many scholars believe that some superstitions have a scientific basis. For example, people in England once used tea made from foxglove plants to treat some forms of heart disease. Today, physicians often prescribe digitalis, a drug made from dried leaves of the purple foxglove, for patients with weak hearts.

10   Some superstitions have a practical origin. For example, many people believe that lighting cigarettes for three individuals from one match will bring bad luck. This superstition may have originated among soldiers during World War I (1914–1918). At night, a match that stayed lit long enough to light three cigarettes provided a target for the enemy. Another superstition involves hanging a bag of garlic around a child's neck for protection from illness. The garlic-filled bag has no supernatural power. But its smell keeps away other children—including any who have a disease that the wearer of the bag might catch.

11   Most people have fears that make them insecure. Superstitions help overcome such fears by providing security. They reassure people that they will get what they want and avoid trouble. For example, millions of people believe in astrology and base important decisions on the position of the sun, moon, planets, and stars. Superstitions will probably have a part in life as long as people fear each other and have uncertainties about the future.

How Well Did You Read?

Complete each sentence with one word to make the statement true.

1. Some people laugh at superstitions because they think superstitions are _____ .

2. Some superstitions have _____ origins.

3. Superstitions may help people deal with their fears by making them feel more _____ .

4. _____ will probably be a part of life for a long time.

ABOVE MATERIAL FROM: FOR YOUR INFORMATION 2

Second Reading

Now read the article again more carefully, paying special attention to the organization.

Understanding the Structure of the Article

An **outline** is an organized analysis of a reading selection. It is often used to help students see the organizational patterns of a reading. Making your own outline of an article will help you understand its basic structure. It will also clarify the relationships between main and supporting ideas.

In the following outline of "Superstition," Roman numerals introduce the general topics, capital letters are used to indicate main ideas, and numbers are used for supporting information. Most of the main ideas in this article are stated in the topic sentence of each paragraph. The main ideas are then supported with specific examples.

Complete the outline.

I. Background Information

    A. Superstition—traditional belief that a certain action or event can cause or foretell an apparently unrelated event.

        1. Carrying a rabbit's foot brings good luck.

        2. _____

        3. _____

    B. _____

    _____

        1. Scholars used to think that all superstitions were very old.

        2. _____

II. Kinds of superstitions

    A. _____

    B. These superstitions ensure that a person will pass safely from one stage of life to the next.

        1. _____

        2. _____

        3. _____

        4. _____

C. _____

    1. _____

    2. _____

    3. Putting money in a wallet before giving it as a gift ensures it will always contain money.

D. Causal superstitions

    1. _____

    2. _____

    3. _____

E. Sign superstitions

    1. _____

    2. _____

    3. _____

    4. _____

    5. _____

Distinguishing Fact from Opinion

Read each statement below. If you think a statement is a fact (something that can be proven), write FC *on the line. If you think it is an opinion (someone's idea), write* OP.

_____ **1.** Doctors often give patients with weak hearts a drug called digitalis.

_____ **2.** Similar actions produce similar results.

_____ **3.** Throughout history, every society has had some forms of superstition.

_____ **4.** Some superstitions have a scientific basis.

_____ **5.** Superstitions will be a part of life as long as people fear each other and the future.

_____ **6.** Not all superstitions date back to man's early history

Application of Information

How superstitious are you? Answer the following questions.

1. If you break a mirror, do you think it brings seven years of bad luck? _____

2. Would you leave for a vacation on Friday the 13th? _____

3. Would you open an umbrella indoors? _____

4. Do you avoid walking under ladders? _____

5. Do you cross your fingers for good luck? _____

6. Do you avoid stepping on cracks? _____

7. Do you believe finding a four-leaf clover is good luck? _____

8. If a black cat crosses your path, do you get upset? _____

9. Do you carry a rabbit's foot for good luck? _____

10. Do you knock on wood to protect yourself against bad luck? _____

11. Do you make a wish if you see a shooting star? _____

12. Do you always enter and leave a house by the same door? _____

13. Do you believe that spilling salt brings bad luck? _____

 **The U. S. Treasury Department stopped printing two-dollar bills because many people considered them unlucky and refused to use them.**

SELECTION 2

Many superstitions involve the belief in lucky and unlucky numbers. **What Will Tomorrow Bring?** discusses some of these numbers and the origins of the superstitions involving them.

Before You Read

Prereading Discussion

1. Many people are superstitious when it comes to choosing a lucky number. Do you have any lucky numbers that you depend on? What are they?

2. How did you choose your lucky numbers and what significance do they have? When do you use them?

What Will Tomorrow Bring?

DANIEL COHEN

1   The next time you ride an elevator in a tall building see if there is a 13th floor. Some buildings have one, but others do not. From the 12th floor, they skip right to the 14th. What happened to the 13th floor? It is there, of course, but it is called 14. In this and similar situations, the number 13 is frequently avoided. The "Devil's dozen"—an old name for 13—is supposed to bring bad luck.

2   There is nothing lucky or unlucky about any number. The belief that a number can bring good or bad luck is a superstition held by a surprisingly large number of people. A superstition is a belief or practice that does not rely on fact but is usually based on fear of the unknown or on ignorance. Most superstitions are supposed to make something good happen or prevent misfortune.

THE 13TH GUEST

3   The 13th day of the month, particularly if it is a Friday, is regarded as unlucky by superstitious people. Many of us joke about Friday the 13th. But others are cautious about their activities on that day for fear that an accident or other disaster may occur. Some superstitious people also consider it unlucky for a group of 13 to eat dinner together. One of them, according to the superstition, will die within a year.

4   We do not know how the number 13 got its bad reputation. "Unlucky 13" may have started with the Vikings or other Norsemen. They told the story of a great banquet for 12 guests—all of them gods. The evil god Loki, angry at not being invited, sneaked into the banquet. Now there were 13 guests. One of the gods at the banquet was killed, and since that time—the story goes—the number 13 has been considered unlucky.

5   Some think the belief started with Christianity. At the Last Supper, there were 13—Jesus Christ and the 12 apostles. The Last Supper was followed by Christ's crucifixion so that, again, the number 13 was identified with a dreadful event. It is believed that Christ was crucified on a Friday. This explains why Friday is regarded by some superstitious people as unlucky. For example, Friday is supposed to be a bad day to start a new job, to begin a voyage, to cut one's nails, or to get married.

YOUR OWN IMAGE

6   "Breaking a mirror brings 7 years' bad luck," goes the old superstition. Of course, it is dangerous to break anything made of glass because you may cut your hand. But there are no superstitious beliefs attached to breaking a drinking glass or a light bulb. The mirror is special because you can see your own image in it.

7   The mirror belief began thousands of years ago, when man thought that his image (picture, sculpture, or reflection) was part of him. He believed, too, that what happened to his image would happen to him.

8   The first mirrors were probably quiet ponds. When a man looked into a pond and saw his image, smooth and unruffled, it was a sign that the gods would be good to him. But if the image was broken and distorted by ripples, there was trouble ahead.

9   Mirror images are clear unless the mirror is cracked. Originally, the image itself was thought to foretell the future. As time passed, the cracked mirror rather than the image became the sign of bad luck.

3 PLUS 4

10   Why is a cracked mirror supposed to cause 7 years' bad luck? Seven is a special number that for thousands of years has meant either good or bad luck. Its supposed magic dates back to early superstitious beliefs about the numbers 3 and 4. Once numbers were more than signs for counting all sorts of quantities. They also represented specific things or ideas.

11   Today we generally do not identify the number 3 with anything in particular; it is used to count books, fruit, bicycles, and so on. But to some ancient peoples, like the Egyptians, the number 3 represented the Mother, Father, and Son. These 3, called a trinity, were regarded as the basis for continuing life from one generation to the next.

12   In time, the number 3 came to represent something more than the continuation of life. Since life was mysterious and spiritual, the number 3 grew to mean the spirit or mind of man.

13   The number 4 represented the 4 chief directions—north, south, east, and west. Earth was then believed to be square. The number 4 and the 4 directions it represented were shown as a small square that looked like a house.

14   Three and 4 were combined to produce the sacred number 7. Small wonder that 7 is connected with so many superstitions! It once stood for an immensely powerful idea: the house that contains the spirit of man.

FYI One out of eight North Americans thinks that Elvis Presley is still alive.

How Well Did You Read?

Read the following statements. If a statement is true, write T *on the line. If it is false, write* F.

_____   **1.** There are several theories about how 13 became an unlucky number.

_____   **2.** The number 13 was once called the Devil's dozen.

_____   **3.** Superstitions are based on scientific facts.

_____   **4.** Starting a new job on a Friday could be a problem for some people who are superstitious.

_____   **5.** Some superstitious people would not want to eat dinner with twelve other guests.

_____   **6.** The superstition that breaking a mirror brings bad luck is very old.

_____   **7.** Seven has been a special number for thousands of years and always means good luck.

_____   **8.** Numbers used to mean more than they do today.

_____   **9.** For some ancient peoples the number 3 had a special significance.

Recalling Information

How much can you remember? Complete the paragraph with information from the article. See how much you can do without referring to the article. Then go back and look up the rest of the answers.

Many people are superstitious about _____. For example, the number _____ is supposed to bring luck. We do not know exactly how it got its bad _____. There are many theories. Some think it may have started with the Vikings. Others think the belief began with _____. _____ is another number that is associated with superstitions. If you break a _____ it is supposed to cause _____ of _____. Ideas about the magic of the number _____ are very old, dating back to superstitions about the numbers _____ and _____. In the past, numbers were more than _____. They represented _____. For instance, the number three meant _____ and the number four represented _____.

Talk it Over

Discussion Questions

1. Summarize the way superstitions about the following numbers may have started.

13 _____

_____

3 _____

_____

4 _____

_____

2. Discuss the origins of the superstition that breaking a mirror brings seven years of bad luck.

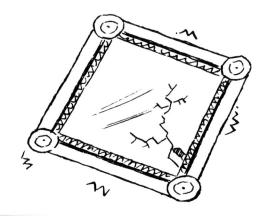

SELECTION 3

An object or a person that supposedly brings bad luck is said to be cursed or jinxed. People who believe in this superstition think that a person, place, object, or even an idea can be jinxed. In **It's Jinxed!**, you will read about a place that was supposed to be jinxed.

It's Jinxed!

DANIEL COHEN

1   Certain objects are supposed to bring good luck, but others have a reputation of being jinxed—that is, of bringing bad luck. The Hope diamond, one of the world's greatest gems, is supposed to bring misfortune to its owners. Today, this jinxed stone is on display in the Smithsonian Institution in Washington, D.C. Its reputation for bad luck does not keep thousands of visitors from flocking to see it every year.

2   Places as well as objects can be jinxed. For example, consider the story of the "Pharaoh's Curse." The rulers, or kings, of ancient Egypt were called pharaohs. In 1922, archaeologists (scientists who study ancient civilizations) made a spectacular discovery in Egypt. They uncovered the tomb of the Pharaoh Tutankhamen, an event that made headlines throughout the world.

3   Shortly after the tomb was opened, three people who had been connected with the expedition died. They all died of different causes, and their deaths were entirely natural. But the coincidence unleashed a flood of stories that the tomb had been cursed.

4   There was a tale that the inscription "Death to those who enter this tomb" was carved above the tomb door. This inscription never existed. Nor did those who believed in the curse ever bother to explain how dozens of others connected with the expedition lived long and successful lives after entering the tomb. The story of the "Pharaoh's Curse" was kept alive in newspapers and magazines for years. In the end, it proved to be one of the biggest hoaxes in the history of superstition.

INVENTION OF A SUPERSTITION

5   Howard Carter and Lord Carnarvon became world famous in 1922 for finding the tomb of the Pharaoh Tutankhamen. When Lord Carnarvon died some months later, the "Pharaoh's Curse" was blamed.

6   The curse was mysterious and awesome—and a fraud. It was invented by reporters who wanted to provide their readers with an exciting story that would continue to sell newspapers and magazines.

7   Like many members of the expedition, Howard Carter—the chief discoverer of the tomb—lived a normal life span. He died in 1939 at the age of 66.

How Well Did You Read?

Read the following statements. If a statement is true, write T on the line. If it is false, write F.

_____ **1.** Since the Hope diamond is supposed to be jinxed, few people want to get near it.

_____ **2.** Both places and objects can have reputations for being jinxed.

_____ **3.** When the tomb of Pharaoh Tutankhamen was discovered, it was written about in newspapers all over the world.

_____ **4.** Three people died from supernatural causes right after the tomb was opened.

_____ **5.** "Death to those who enter this tomb" is written above the door of Pharaoh Tutankhamen's tomb.

_____ **6.** "The Pharaoh's Curse" is one of the biggest hoaxes in the history of superstitions.

Figure it Out

Vocabulary in Context

Without using your dictionary, write an approximate definition or a synonym for the highlighted words in the following sentences.

1. Certain objects are supposed to bring good luck, but others have a reputation of being **jinxed**—that is, of bringing bad luck.

_____

2. Its reputation for bad luck does not keep thousands of visitors from **flocking** to see it every year.

_____

3. In 1922, **archaeologists** (scientists who study ancient civilizations) made a spectacular discovery in Egypt.

_____

4. There was a tale that the **inscription** "Death to those who enter this tomb" was carved above the tomb door.

_____

5. The curse was mysterious and awesome—and a **fraud**. It was invented by reporters who wanted to provide their readers with an exciting story. . . .

_____

6. The rulers, or kings, of ancient Egypt were called **pharaohs.**

_____

ABOVE MATERIAL FROM: FOR YOUR INFORMATION 2

Identifying Main Ideas

The following is a list of main ideas from the article. Locate the paragraph that contains each idea on the list. Write the number of the paragraph on the line provided.

_____ 1. Objects such as the Hope diamond have a reputation of being jinxed.

_____ 2. By coincidence, three people connected with the expedition of Pharaoh Tutankhamen's tomb died.

_____ 3. The story of the "Pharaoh's Curse" proved to be a hoax.

_____ 4. Places like Pharaoh Tutankhamen's tomb can also be jinxed.

Application of Information

Imagine that you were a reporter in 1922. Write a story for your newspaper reporting the discovery of the pharaoh's tomb and the mysterious death of Howard Carter. Be sure to include a headline that would catch your readers' attention.

Postreading Discussion Questions

1. For thousands of years people have believed in superstitions. Why? What are we looking for when we accept superstitions?

2. Something that is "paranormal" is difficult to explain. The paranormal includes belief in superstitions, astrology, magic, faith healers, witchcraft, and others. Do you feel that it is dangerous for people to believe in the paranormal? Why or why not?

3. Do you think that believing in superstitions is unscientific? Do you believe that science can find a satisfactory explanation for everything? Why or why not? Give specific examples to support your answer.

4. Humorist and journalist Don Marquis has observed that "Science has always been too dignified to invent a good back-scratcher." What does this quote mean? Do you agree or disagree with it? What does the quote mean in terms of the debate between science and superstition?

Reader's Journal

Write for ten to twenty minutes in your Reader's Journal about your thoughts on superstitions. Be as specific as you can and give lots of examples to support your ideas.

The Way We Are

SELECTION 1

It's hard to imagine a world without color. Color brings beauty into our lives and influences the way we behave in many subtle ways. **How Color Can Change Your Life** discusses some of the ways that color affects our lives.

Before You Read

Prereading Questions

1. In what ways do colors influence your behavior?

2. Do you have a favorite color for clothing? Do you tend to pick the same kinds of colors when you decorate? If so, what are they?

3. Do you prefer to take color or black-and-white photographs? Why?

How Color Can Change Your Life

You don't have to be Dorothy entering the Land of Oz⋆ for the first time to notice that everything looks better in color. But being aware of colors affects everything from your mood to your appetite. And once you know how they work, you can make them work for you. We drew on the expertise of psychologists, behavioral scientists and marketing researchers to uncover some useful news about hues.

BY PAMELA STOCK

1   You've been in the office all day. Your brain feels deep-fried. You can barely keep your eyes open. There could be a simple explanation for your dipping energy level—not enough bold blue in your life. A study conducted by the University of California at Berkeley showed that prison guards could consistently lift weights longer when facing a

⋆**Dorothy entering the Land of Oz** Refers to the popular movie *The Wizard of Oz,* in which Dorothy, a little girl from Kansas, is whisked away by a tornado to a beautiful, mythical land called Oz. In the film, the Kansas scenes are in black and white. When Dorothy lands in Oz, the film suddenly turns into glorious full color.

How Color Can Change Your Life by Pamela Stock. Published in *Mademoiselle,* August 1994 issue. Courtesy Mademoiselle. Copyright © 1994 by the Condé Nast Publications Inc.

blue poster board than when facing a pink one. So rev up your office walls with artwork that features lots of bright blue: it could help you stay charged if you have to work late. And they might come in handy for an evening softball game—scientists at the University of Texas at Austin found that gazing at a blue light improved athletes' hand-eye coordination.

BEATING STRESS

2　If it's 2 A.M. and you're still tossing and turning over things that happened at work, think pastels. Pink and light blue walls have been shown to lower blood pressure and pulse rates, says health writer Morton Walker, author of *The Power of Color* (Avery, 1990). By hanging up pink or pale blue curtains, you can give yourself a dose of instant calm.

3　Pastels have not cornered the comfort field, however, and if you're feeling stressed to the max, you may find yourself veering to shades of green. Because it is the easiest color for the eye to process, people who are experiencing upheaval in their lives often choose green accessories or housewares, says Cynthia Cornell, the projects coordinator for the Santa Barbara, California-based Wagner Institute for Color Research, a marketing research firm that tracks color trends and performs studies for corporate clients such as Sears, Ford, and Pratt and Lambert Paint. "Those who are drawn to green are often in search of security," she says. Think of it this way—a forest-green throw pillow is a quick, inexpensive and attractive fix.

EATING WELL

4　If you're munching on everything in sight and even the linoleum is starting to look tempting, you should be on the alert—red alert, that is. The color red has been proven to be a stimulant that releases adrenaline, increases the pulse rate, raises blood pressure and enhances appetite, says Walker. Some fast-food restaurants count on bright red walls to encourage speedy eating and ensure a rapid turnover, according to Cornell.

5　If you're having trouble sticking to a diet, you may want to pick a blue color scheme. Research shows that blue reduces appetite, possibly because so few blue foods exist in nature, suggests Walker. Then again, the key may be cultural—market research reveals that people associate blue (and green) with mold.

THE LITTLE BLACK BOX

Black, that wardrobe main-stay is technically not a color at all, but the absorption of all other colors. Culturally, it's long been associated with mourning and depression. An entire office— or as in the case of New York, a whole city—of people wearing black "seems really very sad" says Walker.

People who gravitate to black may be unconsciously unhappy or they could be trying not to be noticed, Walker suggests. Or they could simply be practical and stylish. As Cynthia Cornell advises, "It's important to wear colors you feel comfortable in. We all like black—it makes us feel slender."

GETTING PROMOTED

6　You're excited about starting a new job, and you've decided that your bright red suit will get you noticed. Hold off. You might not be sending the proper message. While small doses of red—such as a scarf or blouse—can be warm and inviting, too much can be overwhelming. And as anyone who's walked through Amsterdam's red-light district knows, the color red screams sex. Instead, go for blue. In the United States, dark blue has historically been associated with power, responsibility and respectability.

7　For contrast, you might give your wardrobe a jolt of yellow. This is the first color that your eye processes, color researchers have discovered, which is why stores use yellow signs to mark sale items. But yellow, like red, is best in small doses—too much has been shown to make people irritable.

8　Keep in mind that color awareness won't make you master of the universe. And you certainly shouldn't feel you have to give up your personal preferences in order to become a savvy color strategist. But color can make a difference—in the end, remember, it was the power of Dorothy's ruby slippers★★ that brought her home safely . . . even if life in Kansas did turn out to be black-and-white.

How Well Did You Read?

Answer the following questions.

1. What color enhances the appetite? Why?

2. What color is the easiest for the eye to process?

3. What color do stores use to indicate sale items? Why?

4. What color reduces the appetite? Why?

5. How should you use red in your wardrobe for work?

6. What is the color dark-blue associated with in the United States?

Building Reading Skills

Understanding Point of View

Put a check mark next to the statements you think the author would agree with.

_____ 1. A red suit with a blue tie would be a better choice for a job interview than a blue suit with a red tie.

_____ 2. If your job is very stressful, light blue would be a good color to choose for your walls.

_____ 3. Pastels are the only colors that are comforting.

_____ 4. The colors you wear can send important messages to others.

_____ 5. If you want to lose weight, it would not be a good idea to use a lot of red when you decorate your kitchen.

_____ 6. If you have trouble staying awake and concentrating on your work, try moving to a place with lots of bright blue.

_____ 7. Color awareness is the most important ingredient for success on the job.

★★Dorothy's ruby slippers In *The Wizard of Oz*, Dorothy wears magical shoes that help her return home to Kansas.

Building Reading Skills

Summarizing

In your own words, summarize the main ideas of "How Color Can Change Your Life."

_____

_____

_____

_____

_____

Figure it Out

Color Idioms

Write a definition for the italicized idioms in the following sentences. Use the context of the sentences to help you figure out the meanings. Then check your definition with a dictionary or your teacher.

1. After staying inside and studying for final exams for three weeks, we decided to go out and *paint the town red* when our last exam was over.

_____

2. We *rolled out the red carpet* for the president of our college when he came to our house for dinner.

_____

3. I can't go to the movies with you tonight. I'm so broke I don't have a *red cent* to my name.

_____

4. The story about the bank president's stealing money was a *red herring* to turn his employees against him.

_____

5. It was a *red-letter day* for Carmen when she won the poetry contest.

_____

6. It took me weeks to change my visa status because there was so much *red tape* involved in the process.

_____

7. Radio is not as popular now as it was in the past. Nowadays, many radio stations operate *in the red* and, unfortunately, may have to stop broadcasting.

_____

8. Paul is never satisfied where he is working. He keeps changing his job because, to him, the grass is *always greener on the other side of the fence.*

_____

9. After a fast and scary ride on a roller coaster, all of the children came home looking *green around the gills.*

_____

10. Alice was *green with envy* when she saw her best friend's beautiful engagement ring.

_____

11. My grandmother always has the most beautiful garden in town. Everyone says she has a *green thumb.*

_____

12. The first time Ben went skate boarding he fell so many times that he came home *black and blue.*

_____

13. All businesses try to be *in the black* at the end of the year.

_____

14. Although Dave didn't like his wife's new haircut, he told a *little white lie* and said that he loved it.

_____

15. I usually buy new bed sheets, pillowcases, and towels at the January *white sale.*

_____

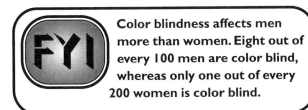

Color blindness affects men more than women. Eight out of every 100 men are color blind, whereas only one out of every 200 women is color blind.

16. We're having a hard time selling our grandparent's old house because it's run down and in a dangerous neighborhood. It's a *white elephant*.

_____

17. Antonio argued with his parents until he was *blue in the face,* but they still wouldn't let him borrow their car for the weekend.

_____

18. It was a *blue Monday,* and the students had a hard time staying awake in class after having had so much fun during the weekend.

_____

19. Pete is so *yellow-bellied* that he avoids anything that takes courage.

_____

20. Yumi started a new routine of exercising daily and eating nutritious food. After a few weeks she felt *in the pink.*

_____

21. Nadya was *tickled pink* when her boyfriend gave her a gold necklace for Valentine's Day

_____

Talk it Over

Discussion Questions

1. The way we feel about different colors is influenced by our culture. What do each of the following colors mean in your culture?

white	blue
black	green
red	yellow

2. Do you have any idiomatic expressions related to color in your language? If so, give some examples.

SELECTION 2

How good are you at handling stress? Humor is one of the best defenses we have against the stress, emotional isolation, and sense of powerlessness that we all feel at one time or another. As you read **Smile If You're Feeling Stressed**, think about the ways that you deal with tension in your life.

Before You Read

Prereading Questions

1. Make a list of the kinds of things that stress you the most. Then share your list with your classmates.

_____

_____

_____

_____

_____

_____

2. Discuss some of the best ways you know of to deal with the various kinds of stress in your life.

Smile If You're Feeling Stressed

Humor is something that in the past was a crisis, but in the present is funny.
—Carol Burnett

BY BRENDA SHOSS

LAUGHTER: THE GREAT PHYSICIAN

1 Anyone who has experienced a gut-busting laugh knows how it interrupts tension. Yet many believe they have to trudge to their serious jobs only to come home to deal seriously with their families. Time out! Where do we get the idea that bosses, kids and spouse won't respect us if we lighten up a little?

2 "Humor is something that in the past was a crisis, but in the present is funny," says comedienne Carol Burnett. In all relationships, at work or home, humor lets people put stressful events in perspective.

Smile if You're Feeling Stressed by Brenda Shoss. Published in the National Safety Council's _Safety & Health Magazine,_ September 1993 issue. Reprinted with the permission of Brenda Shoss.

3   Even large corporations take humor seriously. In a study conducted by Accountemps, 96 percent of executives surveyed think that workers with a sense of humor perform better than those with little or no sense of humor.

4   Laughter also provides physical release from stress. When people laugh, they take deeper breaths. More oxygen means better circulation. Recent studies link laughter to the body's ability to heal. In the book *Anatomy of an Illness*, Norman Cousins cites humor as a way to strengthen the body's own immune system.

5   To date, no one has proved that laughter pills can cure physical problems such as hardening of the arteries. Yet according to Oregon humor writer Jann Mitchell, humor does "stop a hardening of the attitudes in all types of relationships." It is an inexpensive, readily available way to cope with stress.

TYPES OF GOOFBALL BONDING

6   Relationships get into ruts when people forget how to laugh and play. Boring routines, such as housework, can become a source of anger and resentment when couples disagree on who is doing their equal share. Housework takes on a new look when couples wear costumes and scrub to fun music.

7   Humor also brings people together because it is universal. "Laughter is the cement that bonds the group, family or relationship together," say Terry Kellogg and Marvel Harrison in their book, *Finding Balance: 12 Priorities for Interdependence and Joyful Living*. People rarely see things the same way. That's where humor steps in. When two angry people crack up over the same joke, they share a moment of equality. They see each other in a friendlier light.

8   Los Angeles resident John Rennar and his dad frequently travel on business together. While making a hasty exit from a motel parking lot, John drove over what he thought was a speed bump. That bump turned out to be his father's briefcase. Father and son still laugh about the mangled piece of luggage. As a tribute, John's dad created the "Battered Briefcase Award," which he presents annually to the sales rep who commits the most featherbrained act while on the job.

LAUGH OFF TENSION AT WORK

9   "Too many people view their jobs as a five-day prison from which they are paroled every Friday," says Joel Goodman, founder of The Humor Project, a humor-consulting group in Saratoga Springs, N.Y. Humor unlocks the office prison because it lets adults bring some of their childlike spirit to the job.

10   According to Howard Pollio, professor of psychology at the University of Tennessee, Knoxville, an office with "humor breaks" is an office with satisfied and productive employees. Pollio conducted a study that proved humor can help workers excel at routine production tasks. Employees perform better when they have fun.

11   In large corporations with a hierarchy of power, there is often no outlet for stress. "Every company needs underground ways of poking fun at the organization," says Lynn M. Mark, a speaker on workplace humor for St. Mary's Health Center in St. Louis.

12   Kodak's Rochester, N.Y., branch discovered a way for its 20,000 employees to uncork their bottled-up resentments. Their 1,000-squarefoot "Humor Room" features a "toy store." Among the room's many stress-reducing gadgets, the main attraction is a boss doll with Velcro arms and legs. Employees can dismantle the boss, as long as they put its arms and legs back in place.

13   Every April Fool's day, Sun Microsystems of Mountain View, Calif., concocts an intricate hoax aimed at one of its employees. One year, CEO Scott McNealy's office was decorated as a one-hole, par-four miniature golf course. The annual gag does so much for encouraging teamwork and boosting morale that the company has set aside an April Fool's hoax budget.

14   Sandy Cohen, owner of a graphic print-production business, created "The Quote Board" to document the bizarre phrases people say when under strict deadlines. "When you're under stress, you say stupid things," says Cohen. "Now we just look at each other and say, 'That's one for the Quote Board!'"

JUMP ON THE LAUGH TRACK

15   At work or home, the basic tenet for humor is: Take your responsibilities seriously, but don't take yourself so seriously.

- Figure out what makes you grin. To find your funny bone, start a humor file. Write down jokes, cartoons and real-life situations that are a personal hoot. After a while, you'll learn to recognize your own brand of silliness.
- Plan play time. A pet can be a great spontaneous playmate. "After a stressful day, I play with my dog, Charlie. Soon, I'm talking in goofy voices and laughing like a kid," says Samantha from Boston.

  For those who are not quite sure what "play time" means, try these suggestions: Keep a box of crayons on hand. Go to a comedy club instead of a movie. Dance in your living room to your favorite music. Try a new sport. Red-ink a big "me" on your calendar page to remind yourself to schedule play time.
- Adults in toyland. Toys remind grownups that they are still part kid. Mitchell, the Oregon humorist, surrounds herself with toys at the office and at home. When Mitchell has trouble thinking at work, she dons a gold plastic crown. She then parades around her office until a fresh idea hits her.

GIGGLES ON THE ROAD

16 Psychologist Beth Rom-Rymer agrees that laughter is a way to relieve stress—even in your car. She suggests that strained drivers pop a comedy cassette into their car's tape deck when they're stuck in irritating traffic snarls. Instead of listening to those same old radio commercials, try the humor of Bill Cosby or Jerry Seinfeld to relieve a little tension. Don't laugh too hard, though. The driver in front of you might not see the humor in a rear-end collision!

How Well Did You Read?

Read the following statements. If a statement is true, write T *on the line. If it is false, write* F.

_____ **1.** Humor helps people put stressful events in perspective.

_____ **2.** Large corporations do not take humor seriously.

_____ **3.** Laughter provides a physical release from stress.

_____ **4.** Humor can help keep relationships exciting.

_____ **5.** There is no place for humor in the workplace.

FYI Twenty seconds of hearty laughter gives the body the same kind of workout as three minutes of vigorous exercise. Typically, blood pressure drops and muscles relax.

Building Reading Skills

Examining Support

The author mentions several areas of life in which humor can be helpful. List them below and explain how humor helps relieve stress in each area.

a. _____

_____

b. _____

_____

c. _____

_____

d. _____

_____

e. _____

_____

Expanding Vocabulary

Synonyms or Antonyms

Decide if the following pairs of words are synonyms or antonyms. If they are synonyms, circle the S. If they are antonyms, circle the A.

1.	grin	frown	S	A
2.	tension	stress	S	A
3.	mangled	battered	S	A
4.	gag	joke	S	A
5.	bizarre	strange	S	A
6.	spontaneous	planned	S	A
7.	giggle	laugh	S	A
8.	hasty	leisurely	S	A
9.	irritating	unpleasant	S	A
10.	dons	puts on	S	A

Read and React

Discuss the following quotes from the article with your classmates. Then choose one and describe a personal story that proves its truth for you.

1. Humor is something that in the past was a crisis, but in the present is funny.

2. Humor also brings people together because it is universal.

3. Laughter is the cement that bonds the group, family or relationship together.

4. Every company needs underground ways of poking fun at the organization.

5. At work or home, the basic tenet for humor is: Take your responsibilities seriously, but don't take yourself too seriously.

Talk it Over

Discussion Questions

Read and discuss the following statements.

1. Humor does not translate well. It is the first thing that gets lost in a foreign language.

2. Humor breaks down emotional boundaries.

3. If you don't have a sense of humor, you probably don't have any sense at all.

SELECTION 3

Aging is the process of growing old. For most of us, the process of aging begins sometime between the ages of thirty and forty. Heredity and environment both play a role in the way that we age. **Brain Power's Sliding Scale** and its sidebar "Use It or Lose It?" present research into the process of aging and examine how it may work differently in men and women.

Before You Read

Prereading Activity

Read the statements below and decide whether you agree or disagree with each one. Discuss your opinions with your classmates.

1. Women are generally better at verbal skills.

2. The brains of men and women are anatomically different.

3. There are dramatic differences between the way male and female brains age.

4. Older people have a greater range of intellectual ability than younger people.

5. Women's spatial skills start to decline before men's.

Brain Power's Sliding Scale

Aging

BY JUDY FOREMAN

"Most of the data I have looked at don't show dramatic differences between men and women. They are there, and they are real, but relative to the impact of other things, they are fairly small."

Richard Mohs, Psychologist,
Bronx Veterans Affairs Medical Center

1   You would think Harvard psychologist Douglas Powell, 60, would be the last to worry that he was "losing it."

2   After all, he has spent years concocting tests to see which skills—such as attention, visuospatial ability, verbal fluency and memory—slip most with normal aging.

3   In fact, Powell is writing a book on normally aging minds and runs a company that helps hospitals determine if the minds of their oldest doctors are still intact.

4   Yet one day recently, right after being interviewed about mental aging, Powell stopped to put gas in his car and left the gas cap on the trunk. A clear sign, or so he says, of attention deficit, a particular plague for aging men.

5   When he got home, a rattled Powell told his wife Virginia, "I am a wreck. I was talking to the *Globe* about what you lose. This is the second time in a row I've lost the gas cap on the trunk of my car. I'm really losing it."

6   Virginia, also 60 and CEO of their consulting company, was unfazed, noting in wifely fashion that in some ways—like searching for the glasses on top of his head—he had always been this way.

7   It is but small comfort, Powell says, that, in lockstep with his attentional abilities, his wife's map-reading skills have also declined, as visuospatial skills of older women often do.

8   With the passing years, Powell, like many of the rest of us, finds himself ever quicker to pounce on evidence of mental slippage. And like many a couple, the Powells sometimes think they see gender differences in the foibles of aging minds.

9   But whether such differences in fact exist, and how important they may be, are very much open questions, questions often pursued, curiously enough, by husband-and-wife research teams.

10   The bottom line is that even where gender differences in cognitive aging exist, the effects are probably small. Education, for instance, is by far a more powerful predictor of mental function in later life, notes Richard Mohs, a psychologist at the Bronx Veterans Affairs Medical Center who studies aging and memory as part of a $25 million effort by the Charles A. Dana Foundation in New York.

11   "Most of the data sets I have looked at don't show dramatic differences between men and women," Molis says. "They are there, and they are real, but relative to the impact of other things, they are fairly small."

12   Still, the more researchers wade into the intellectual—and often political—swamp of gender differences, the more they find small differences in the way male and female brains age.

13   In studies of 200 men and women aged 30 to 80, for instance, Dr. Marilyn Albert, director of gerontology research at Massachusetts General Hospital, has found that women decline faster than men at some spatial tasks, though she stresses that far more noticeable are changes in memory, "executive functions" like planning and problem-solving, and recalling names. All those abilities decline with age in both sexes at the same rate.

Brain Power's Sliding Scale by Judy Foreman. Published in the *Boston Globe,* May 16,1994. Reprinted courtesy of the *Boston Globe.*

ABOVE MATERIAL FROM: FOR YOUR INFORMATION 3

14   At Pennsylvania State University, K. Warner Schaie and his wife Sherry Willis, both professors of human development, have studied about 5,000 people—some of them for as long as 35 years—through the Seattle Longitudinal Study, a project Schaie started in 1956 at the University of Washington.

15   Overall, they find, men lose mental skills faster than women, perhaps because at any given age, as Schaie put it in a telephone interview, men are "closer to death."

16   But for many men, skills such as spatial orientation, which is often seen as a male strength, hold up well into the 80s.

17   By contrast, he says, women's spatial ability—often seen as a comparative weakness—declines about twice as much as men's.

18   Schaie, who defines spatial skills as being able to do such things as look at a map and determine which way to turn, or to assemble furniture that comes in pieces, discussed such gender differences in an April article in the *American Psychologist.*

19   Men and women, he finds, decline at about the same rate on inductive reasoning, when tested on such tasks as figuring out the underlying principle in railroad schedules (for example, that a train leaves every hour at 17 minutes past the hour). But because women start out better, they tend to keep this edge into late life, Schaie says.

20   Women also maintain a lifelong advantage at verbal comprehension (recognizing vocabulary), verbal memory (recalling lists of words) and word fluency (generating lists of words that start with a certain letter, for instance).

21   For both men and women, Schaie emphasizes, the most striking thing about aging minds is that the range of intellectual ability is greater among older people than among younger ones. And for both sexes, he adds, the rule of thumb is that people retain the skills they use in daily life and tend to lose the ones they do not practice. "And in reality," he says, "you can't practice everything."

22   Verbal skills are often well-maintained precisely because most people keep using them, he says, though even for women verbal comprehension declines in the 80s, probably because by this age women are widowed and have less opportunity to talk to someone.

23   Like other researchers, Douglas Powell has found that although women's spatial skills start to slide before men's, both sexes lose mental skills in a distinct order: visuospatial first, then reasoning, then verbal memory. Along with Sandra Weintraub, head of neuropsychology at Beth Israel Hospital, Powell has studied 1,000 physicians, most of them men age 25 to 60, and 600 other men and women.

24   Gail Hochanadel, a psychologist who works with her husband, Paul Spiers, at Neuropsychology Associates in Topsfield, has studied 42 volunteers from the Framingham Heart Study, looking not just at overall test scores but at the kinds of errors that were made.

25   "The type of error can tell us what area of the brain is involved, not just whether performance is impaired," she says.

26   Her error analysis showed that both men and women suffer age-related declines in frontal lobe function, the area of the brain important for "executive" duties such as planning and juggling tasks that have to be done at the same time.

27   But while men's decline begins in the 70s, she finds, "women didn't show it until their 80s."

28   Unlike some researchers, Hochanadel also finds that in their 70s, men also begin to show more errors in right hemisphere function, where spatial tasks are performed. Perhaps, she speculates, the decline in levels of the male hormone, testosterone, in aging men may trigger a decline in spatial abilities.

29   (While there is little data on male hormones and brain function, growing but still-inconclusive data suggest that in women, taking the female hormone estrogen after menopause reduces the risk of Alzheimer's and boosts verbal memory.)

30   Edith Kaplan, associate professor of neurology and psychiatry at Boston University School of Medicine, offers an explanation of the relative mental losses in men and women.

31   Throughout life, she says, men's and women's brains are anatomically different, with women having a thicker *corpus callosum*—a network of fibers—connecting the two hemispheres.

32   Because of the interconnections, she says, it may be easier for women to use their still-strong verbal skills to compensate for declining visuospatial skills.

33   But there is, Kaplan adds, one tactic both sexes can easily use to stay sharp: social interaction, which, research suggests, can help keep a number of cognitive skills intact.

34   Hochanadel strongly agrees: "Party on! It's good for you."

JUDY FOREMAN is a member of the Boston Globe staff.

USE IT OR LOSE IT?

Researchers disagree whether the "use it or lose it" philosophy holds for cognitive aging, but there is some evidence that keeping mentally active can slow age-related declines.

At Pennsylvania State University, Sherry Willis and her husband, K. Warner Schaie, have studied 5,000 people, some since 1956. People lucky enough to avoid chronic diseases may also fare better in intellectual function, they find, perhaps because chronic diseases can restrict lifestyle and reduce mental stimulation. Similarly, those lucky enough to be relatively affluent also fare better, perhaps because money can buy intellectually stimulating things like travel.

Education helps, too, researchers say, perhaps because it instills the conviction that you can always learn something new. The Schaie-Willis team also has some other observations. Being in a stable marriage with a stimulating spouse, they say, helps maintain intellectual vigor.

Flexibility counts, too. People who stay mentally vibrant are often those who do not insist that "they must do things today as they did before," Schaie says. In neuropsychological terms, the ability to see problems in new ways often yields higher scores on tests of mental function. And people satisfied with life also stay more mentally fit, he says.

If you find your mental skills sagging, consider working on specific deficits. When Willis gave 5-hour tutorials on inductive reasoning or spatial skills to about 200 people whose skills had declined in the previous 14 years, 40 percent regained lost abilities. That advantage held up seven years later when they were re-tested.

Other ways to stay sharp, Schaie says, are doing jigsaw puzzles to hone visuo-spatial skills, working crossword puzzles for verbal skills, playing bridge for memory and simply matching wits at home with players on TV game shows.

Finally, remember this. Even though you may lose some mental skills with normal aging, you also gain in one key area: wisdom.

At Harvard Medical School, Dr. Marsel Mesulain and Changiz Geula speculate that the growth in wisdom—loosely defined as the maturation of intellectual abilities that comes with life experience—may be linked to the fact that nerve fibers in the brain's association cortex, which integrates different forms of knowledge, continue to be newly myelinated throughout the 40s, 50s and even 60s. Myelination is the process by which nerves are covered with a protective coating, which speeds up neural communication.

The Harvard team has also found that, unlike some other brain chemicals, one called AChE (acetylcholinesterase) continues to be made late in adult life in the "pyramidal" neurons in the cortex, or outer layers of the brain. High levels of AChE in these cells, they speculate, may be associated with the increasing wisdom in later life.

By Judy Foreman

Evaluating Your Opinions

Look back at the statements in the prereading section on page 121. Have any of your opinions changed since you read "Brain Power's Sliding Scale"? If so, which ones?

How Well Did You Read?

Answer the following questions based on information from the article and its sidebar.

1. As people grow older, what kinds of skills do they usually retain? Give a specific example to support your answer.

2. In what order do both sexes lose their mental skills?

3. What is one reason that women may be able to use their strong verbal skills to compensate for declining visuospatial skills as they grow older?

4. According to researchers, what factors help prevent age-related mental decline?

5. What are some examples of specific activities that can help prevent mental decline?

_____

_____

_____

Building Reading Skills

Fact Versus Theory

Read the following statements. If according to the article a statement is a fact (something that has been proven), write FACT on the line. If according to the article a statement is a theory (someone's idea or assumption that has not yet been proven), write THEORY on the line.

_____ **1.** Keeping mentally active can slow age-related mental declines.

_____ **2.** Nerve fibers in the association cortex of the brain continue to be myelinated throughout middle age.

_____ **3.** Being in a stable marriage with a stimulating spouse helps maintain intellectual functioning.

_____ **4.** The brains of men and women are anatomically different.

_____ **5.** There are definite, but small, gender differences in the way brains age.

_____ **6.** Education, chronic illness, and standard of living all affect cognitive aging.

_____ **7.** The frontal lobe of the brain manages tasks that have to be done at the same time.

> **FYI**
>
> One out of every 2.1 billion people lives to be 115 years old.

Figure it Out

Idioms

Look back through the article and underline each of the following idiomatic expressions. Then, using context from the paragraph and the sentences provided, write a definition for each one. Finally, write your own sentence that expresses the meaning of the idiom.

1. in a row (¶5)

I'm sure I'll get a good grade in this course. I've gotten As on the last three tests _in a row._

definition: _____

sentence: _____

2. the bottom line (¶10)

Jason is having a lot of trouble in his calculus course. Although he is trying very hard, *the bottom line* is that he needs private tutoring.

definition: _____

sentence: _____

3. put it (¶15)

Madeline *put it* so well when she said that laughter is the best medicine.

definition: _____

sentence: _____

4. hold up (¶16)

Our good luck *held up* for the whole season, and we won every soccer game.

definition: _____

sentence: _____

5. figure out (¶19)

Karen couldn't *figure out* how to use her new computer program.

definition: _____

sentence: _____

6. rule of thumb (¶21)

As a *rule of thumb,* you should drink lots of liquids on hot days.

definition: _____

sentence: _____

Building Writing Skills

Paraphrasing

Rewrite the sentences below using your own words. Your sentences should express the main idea of the original sentences as clearly and simply as possible.

1. With the passing years, Powell, like many of the rest of us, finds himself ever quicker to pounce on evidence of mental slippage.

_____

_____

2. Still, the more researchers wade into the intellectual—and often political—swamp of gender differences, the more they find small differences in the way male and female brains age.

_____

_____

3. For many men, skills such as spatial orientation, which is often seen as a male strength, hold up well into the 80s.

_____

_____

4. For both sexes, . . . the rule of thumb is that people retain the skills they use in daily life and tend to lose the ones they do not practice.

_____

_____

Proverbs

Read and discuss the following sayings about aging. Think of some more to add to the list.

1. Better to wear out than to rust out.
2. You are never too old to learn.
3. They that live longest, see the most.
4. Young folks think that old folks are fools.
5. Youth is wasted on the young.
6. You're only as old as you feel.

_____

_____

_____

_____

ABOVE MATERIAL FROM: FOR YOUR INFORMATION 3

TYING IT ALL TOGETHER

Word Forms

A. *Complete the chart by filling in the missing forms of the words. The verb forms have been given.*

Verb	Noun	Adjective	Adverb
behave			
comfort			
coordinate			
encourage			
flex			
relate			
resent			
respect			
speculate			
theorize			

B. *Complete the sentences with words from the chart.*

1. Even though I disagree with you, I _____ your opinions.

2. Although black holes in the universe _____ exist, no one has ever seen one.

3. Kazuo is the _____ of all of the special programs.

4. A good coach gives his team a lot of _____ .

5. Doctors believe there is a _____ between stress and head colds.

6. We can visit you any time this weekend; our plans are pretty _____ .

7. Since we can't predict the future, we can only _____ about what will happen next.

8. Five people can fit _____ in our new car.

9. Julie felt great _____ toward her sister for stealing her boyfriend.

10. The children were punished for their bad _____ during math class.

Reader's Journal

Choose a topic that relates to the readings in this unit and write for about ten to twenty minutes. Consider writing about one of the quotes in this unit or answering one of the discussion questions.

WRITING SECTION

UNIT 9

Problem/Solution

Modelo

When your purpose is to describe a problem and evaluate possible solutions, use a **problem/solution pattern of organization**. For example, if you are discussing solutions to the problem of employee dissatisfaction in your company or the problems of adjusting to a foreign culture, you would use this type of organization. You should organize your solutions according to order of importance.

The problem/solution pattern is very useful in academic writing. For example, you would use it in a sociology class if you were asked to describe the problem of overpopulation and offer several solutions. You could also use this pattern in an economics class if you needed to analyze the problem of unemployment and suggest some ways to solve it.

Examining Solutions

For each of the problems described below, think of at least three possible solutions. Work in small groups and then compare your solutions with those of your classmates.

1. Living in a foreign country can be fun and exciting, but it can also be problematic. One of the most serious problems that people living in a foreign country face is culture shock. What ways can you think of to help people deal with this problem?

PROBLEM: Culture shock

SOLUTIONS: a. _____

   b. _____

   c. _____

2. Many people have trouble falling asleep or staying asleep for an adequate amount of time. This problem is known as insomnia. What suggestions would you give to people who cannot seem to get a good night's sleep?

PROBLEM: Insomnia

SOLUTIONS: a. _____

b. _____

c. _____

3. Stress at work or school can be a serious problem. A person suffering from too much stress usually finds it difficult to be productive or happy. What are some ways to reduce the amount of stress in someone's life?

PROBLEM: Stress at work or school

SOLUTIONS: a. _____

b. _____

c. _____

4. The population of the world keeps growing. Every 15 seconds, approximately 100 babies are born. Experts predict that by the year 2000, there could be 6 billion people on our planet. By the end of the next century, the population could reach 10 billion people. The problem is that there probably won't be enough food to feed everyone. What solutions can you come up with to help solve this problem?

PROBLEM: Overpopulation

SOLUTIONS: a. _____

b. _____

c. _____

ABOVE MATERIAL FROM: READY TO WRITE MORE

5. Crime is a serious problem in many large cities. Is crime a serious problem in the large cities in your native country? What solutions can you think of to reduce the amount of crime?

PROBLEM: Crime in large cities in the United States (or another country)

SOLUTIONS: a. _____

b. _____

c. _____

6. Illiteracy is a serious problem all over the world. For example, one-third of adult Americans are functionally illiterate. People who cannot read and write have many disadvantages functioning in society. What solutions can you come up with to help overcome this problem?

PROBLEM: Illiteracy

SOLUTIONS: a. _____

b. _____

c. _____

7. Many of the Earth's resources are nonrenewable and will eventually run out. In order to make our valuable natural resources last longer, we need to conserve materials and recycle them as much as possible. Unfortunately, it is not always easy to convince people of the necessity of recycling. What ideas do you have about getting people to recycle?

PROBLEM: Getting people to recycle

SOLUTIONS: a. _____

b. _____

c. _____

Practicing Solutions

You are the advice consultant for a newspaper. How would you respond to the following letter? Be sure to offer several solutions to each problem in your response. Share your responses by exchanging papers with your classmates or by reading them out loud.

Dear Advisor,

     I am a sophomore in college. Last year my roommate, Fred, and I were very good friends. I don't know what happened, but this year everything has changed. Fred seems really different. He has a whole new group of friends and spends all of his time with them. He stays out late at night and often doesn't get up in time for his classes. He never studies any more and he got kicked off the wrestling team for missing so many practices. He is always either sleeping or out with his new friends. When he is in our room, he is moody, messy, and undependable. Please tell me what to do. I've tried talking to him, but he just tells me to mind my own business. I'm concerned that he is going to get kicked out of school. He is already on academic probation. What should I do?

                        A Concerned Roommate

Dear Concerned,

_____

_____

_____

_____

_____

_____

ABOVE MATERIAL FROM: READY TO WRITE MORE

Analyzing a Problem/Solution Essay

Read the essay below and answer the questions that follow.

Energy Sources: A Dilemma for the Twenty-First Century

All of us have come to expect that reliable sources of energy will be available forever. We drive our cars wherever and whenever we want. When the gas tank gets low, we simply pull into the nearest gas station. At home, whenever we need to change the temperature, prepare food, listen to music, or watch TV, we simply turn on the nearest appliance. What is the source of all this energy that we use so carelessly? In most of the world, energy is created by burning fossil fuels—coal, natural gas, and oil. The problem is that these resources are finite. At our current rate of use, we will be out of petroleum in 30 to 40 years. That means that if you are under the age of 40, the day will probably come when you will not have gasoline for your car or electricity for your appliances. The three most commonly proposed solutions to this worldwide problem are increasing the efficiency of appliances and vehicles, improving conservation efforts, and finding alternative energy sources.

The first solution, improving the efficiency of appliances and vehicles, is something that manufacturers have been working on for two decades. For instance, televisions now use 65 to 75 percent less electricity than they did in the 1970s, refrigerators use 20 to 30 percent less electricity, and cars need less gas to travel more miles. Unfortunately, there are so many more televisions, refrigerators, and cars in the world now that overall consumption continues to rise.

Another solution to the dangerous energy situation is to improve our conservation efforts. For example, all of us must get in the habit of recycling whatever we can. We have to install high-efficiency lightbulbs in our homes and offices and turn off the lights in rooms that we are not using. It would also help if we biked, walked, carpooled, or used public transportation more and used our cars less. Unfortunately, improvements in both conservation and efficiency are only temporary solutions. They extend the useful life of our current fuels, but they do not explain what we will do when these fuels run out.

The best solution, then, is to find alternative sources of energy to meet our future needs. The current leading alternatives to fossil fuels are fusion and solar energy. Fusion is a nuclear reaction that results in an enormous release of energy. It is practically pollution-free and is probably our best long-range option. Unfortunately, it will not be available for at least 20 years. The other possible energy source, solar power, is really the source of all energy, except nuclear, on Earth. When people think of solar energy, they generally think of the many ways that individual homeowners can utilize the power of the sun for heating water and buildings. But solar energy can also be utilized to generate electricity and to purify fuels for automobiles.

It is clear that for us to have sufficient energy resources for the twenty-first century, it will be necessary to pursue the development and encourage the use of alternative energy sources worldwide. If we ignore this problem, what will become of our children? What will life be like for them in the year 2050?

Energy Sources: A Dilemma for the 21st century by Alan Bronstein. Reprinted with permission.

Pair Work

Answer the following questions with a partner:

1. What is the thesis statement of the essay?
2. What three solutions to the energy shortage does the author propose?
3. What examples does the author use to describe each solution?
4. How are the body paragraphs arranged?
5. What technique(s) did the author use in writing the conclusion?

Essay Plan: Problem/Solution

The guidelines below will help you remember what you need to do in each part of a problem/solution essay.

INTRODUCTION
1. Provide background information about the problem.
2. Describe the problem and state why it is serious.
3. Identify possible solutions.

SUPPORTING PARAGRAPHS
1. Discuss one solution in each supporting paragraph.
2. Explain the positive and negative aspects of each solution.
3. Provide details to explain each solution.
4. Organize the paragraphs according to order of importance.

CONCLUSION
1. Summarize the solutions.
2. Draw a conclusion or make a prediction based on your suggestions.

Writing a Problem/Solution Essay

In this activity, you will practice writing an essay that analyzes the solutions to a problem. Follow these steps:

a. Prewriting

Choose one of the following topics and freewrite about it for 10 minutes. Use a separate piece of paper if you do not have enough room here.

1. Sexism
2. The generation gap
3. War
4. Smog
5. Racism

b. Planning

Use your freewriting as a basis for planning your essay. Identify several of your solutions that you think you can develop into an essay. If you have not generated enough ideas, do another, more focused freewriting. Then prepare an informal outline of your essay.

c. Drafting

On a separate piece of paper, write the first draft of your essay. Refer to the essay plan on page 138 to help you with your draft. Be sure to provide some background information on the problem in the introduction and include a clear thesis statement. Organize the body paragraphs according to order of importance, beginning or ending with the most important solution. End with a conclusion that summarizes the solutions, draws a conclusion, or makes a prediction.

d. Personal Revising

Be sure that all your paragraphs are unified and coherent. Also, check to make sure you have provided enough support to explain each solution fully. Write or type a revised version of your essay.

e. Peer Revising

Exchange papers with a classmate. Read your partner's essay and use the following questions to help you with the revision process:

1. What are some interesting things you learned from reading this essay?
2. Did the introduction provide enough background information to explain the problem?
3. How many solutions did the author offer in the essay? Is each solution adequately developed in a separate body paragraph?
4. Are the paragraphs arranged in a logical order? What type of order did the author use?
5. Did the author use transitions to guide you from one idea to the next? Were there any irrelevant sentences that should be eliminated?
6. Did the author include a conclusion that summarizes the solutions or makes a prediction?

Incorporate any suggestions your classmate has made that you agree with.

f. Editing

Correct all the grammar, punctuation capitalization, and spelling errors before you copy it over or type it.

You Be the Editor

The following paragraph contains seven mistakes. Find the mistakes and correct them. Then copy the corrected paragraph onto a separate sheet of paper.

If you are like most people, you average one to three colds per year. Even if you do not have a cold right now. The chances are three in four that within the next year, at least one cold virus will find you. then you'll spend a week or so suffering from the miseries of the common cold: fatigue, sore throat, laryngitis, sneezing, stuffy or runny nose, and coughing. According to researchers, colds are the most common medical reason for missing school and work. Once you catch a cold, what can you do. There is no known cure yet for a cold. There are, however, several thing you can do to suppress the symptom's so that you feel better while the virus runs its course. For example, make sure that you get plenty of sleep and drink lots of liquids. You may find commercially available cold remedies such as decongestants, cough suppressants, and expectorants helpful, but keep in mind that these products can cause side effects. Many people prefer home remedies such as chicken soup, garlic, and ginger tea. In treating a cold, remember the wisdom of the ages, "if you treat a cold, it will be gone in a week; if you don't treat it, will be gone in seven days."

Source: *Jane Brody's Cold and Flu Fighter*

On Your Own

Write a problem/solution essay based on one of the problems you analyzed in the Examining Solutions section on pages 133–135. Be sure your essay has an introduction that describes the problem, several body paragraphs that explain the solutions, and a conclusion that summarizes the solutions or makes a prediction.